COLLECTED BOYHOOD WORKS
Volume Two

BOOK OF KNOWLEDGE AND GREAT UNDERSTANDING

REFLECTIONS ON SCHOOL LIFE

Udenta O. Udenta

Published by

Kraft Books Limited
6A Polytechnic Road, Sango, Ibadan
Box 22084, University of Ibadan Post Office
Ibadan, Oyo State, Nigeria
✆ + 234 (0)803 348 2474, + 234 (0)805 129 1191
E-mail: kraftbooks@yahoo.com
Website: www.kraftbookslimited.com

© Udenta O. Udenta, 2015

First published 2015

ISBN 978-978-918-227-5 (Paperback)
ISBN 978-978-918-279-4 (Hardback)

= KRAFTGRIOTS =
(A literary imprint of Kraft Books Limited)

All Rights Reserved

First printing, February 2015

Author's Note

The volume two of these collected boyhood works contains two materials: *"Book of Knowledge and Great Understanding"* and *"Reflections on School Life."* The first work is a collection of extracts from works that made a great impression on me, particularly Obi. B Egbuna's *The Diary of a Homeless Prodigal*. There are also echoes from other sources I cannot presently recollect. The piece also contains my original philosophical reflections on life and commentary on social and moral issues.

The second material that makes up the volume is a near comprehensive account of secondary school life from the standpoint of a maturing student with developing creative and artistic consciousness.

The two works in this volume were written between 1977 and 1979 when I was 13 – 15 years, just like the rest of the works that make up the other volumes.

Udenta O. Udenta
Abuja
February, 2014

Think! Think!! Think!!!

"Be one of the thinking men, great thinkers and possess the golden qualities of those inventive geniuses."

LAWRENCE KILL-MASTER DENTUS,
DEPARTMENT OF LITTOLOGY AND PHILOSOPHY.
AN ENQUIRY INTO OBSCURITY AND THE NATURE OF LAXITY IN MAN.

"KNOWLEDGE IS POWER."

"SUCCESS IS OURS."

"BOOK OF KNOWLEDGE AND GREAT UNDERSTANDING."

Contents

Author's Note 5
Think! Think! Think! 6
General Introduction to the Volumes 8

1. Book of Knowledge and Great Understanding
Lesson One 27
Lesson Two 30
Lesson Three 34
Lesson Four 36
Lesson Five 39

2. Reflections on School Life
Chapter One 45
Chapter Two 49
Chapter Three 54
Chapter Four 58
Chapter Five 62
Chapter Six 68
Chapter Seven 72
Chapter Eight 79
Chapter Nine 82
Chapter Ten 86
Chapter Eleven 91
Chapter Twelve 95
Chapter Thirteen 100
Chapter Fourteen 104

General Introduction to the Volumes

I have thought long and hard about publishing these volumes of short stories, novels, drama sketches, essays, philosophical musings and other materials of an inter-generic nature written between 1977 and 1979, when I was in high school. All the works in these six volumes were written when I was between the ages of 13 and 15. On very many occasions in the past, I have dismissed the thought of ever publishing these materials, rightly considering them immature, full of linguistic, structural and stylistic inadequacies and, thus capable of sending the wrong kind of signal to better equipped and far more talented teenagers about how best not to nurse, conceive and execute their creative impulses and inspiration.

However, I am now more than convinced that these works should see the light of day, precisely because they meant much to me when they were written, and may be much more now as I cast my mind back to the socio-cultural and spatio-temporal determinations in which they inher. I am also persuaded that my bad English, bad grammar and immature ideas and vision are not an exception to the creative enterprise and pursuits of young people of my age when I wrote them; and that given the opportunities and possibilities open to me, and the obstacles I have had to overcome in creating them, their own creative productions may not be too far higher or lower than my effort.

It will be thus necessary to situate these works within the context of my historical, social, cultural and other sources of identity and motivations, believing that a glimpse into these currents will help place them in their proper and objective psycho-social setting.

My father, Chief Benedict Ikenche Udenta, who died in 2004,

was a trained teacher whose vacation job was to help his elder brothers tap and sell palm wine. By dint of hard work, unique talent and special intellectual gift and drive, he was able to finish his teachers training programme at the famous St. Charles College, Onitsha, Nigeria, earned a Teacher Grade One Certificate subsequently and completed his B.Sc. Inter from the University of London in 1963 or thereabout, the very year I was born.

He broke away from the mission school system because of its overbearing and constricting spiritual-dogmatic conditions, codes and circumstances, which he felt hampered and limited his intellectual growth and liberal disposition and philosophy; taught in a number of secondary and commercial colleges; helped in starting and sustaining the tradition of publishing at Tabansi Publishing Ltd that flourished in the 1960s; wrote and published nearly 20 books; contested for the Federal House of Representatives for the Awgu-Oji River Federal Constituency under the banner of the Dr. K.O. Mbadiwe-led Democratic People's National Congress (DPNC) in 1959; bought a Volkswagen Beetle convertible car that helped in many a local wedding; and erected a storey building in 1963. He made all these accomplishments when he was about 32 or 33 years.

My mother, Madam Pauline Ijeabalum Udenta, who is still alive, complemented my father in virtually all respects. She trained as nurse/midwife at the famous Bishop Shanaham School of Nursing and Midwifery, Nsukka, Nigeria, and practiced for a while in government health institutions before her husband's "opposition politics" in DPNC forced her out of government service into private practice, a calling that she still responds to till date. Her greatest strength is her profound understanding and accommodation of her husband's intellectual and creative disposition and her complete tolerance, love and support for him in the pursuit of what may have then appeared a strange cause. Till the very end of his life, even as his health failed, still struggling gallantly with his reading, research and writing (he became increasingly attracted to mystical philosophy in the last decade and half of his life, essentially as an intellectual pursuit, and not as a devotee, though he compiled by hand and typed over 500 spiritual and mystical prayers for the family), she never ceased to encourage him, though would occasionally take the books and papers away and direct his minds to other things, more so as he found a particular joy in reading the Catholic publication, **Preparation for Death,** in the months leading to his passing away.

The combination of a thoroughly intellectual, even philosophic father who wrote the bulk of his books between his mid-twenties and early thirties, and a very intelligent mother who became increasingly anchored on the same path of social liberalism and tolerance of contrary viewpoints, eventually produced four children who expressed their individual creativity and intellectual consciousness in various ways. Because of their years of travels in places far and wide in the old Anambra State of Nigeria, the children never had the consciousness of growing up in our ancestral, rural village of Mgbowo in Awgu L.G. of Enugu State, Nigeria before the end of the civil war in 1970.

It was thus to this village setting that we journeyed towards the end of 1969, across strange places and lands, on foot and with varied, interesting and exciting, though frightening experiences, to aid our passage. The rest of the family traveled first, while our father followed later, after creating safe passages for us across the hostile, twisting routes with messages of our coming delivered ahead to his comrades in the Biafran Organization of Freedom Fighters (BOFF), an irregular, guerilla army, that became the backbone of the Biafran resistance even after the conventional fighting force had disintegrated, but a force which was under-funded and under-appreciated by a military command structure that seemed completely uninformed about the tactics and strategies of an unconventional warfare.

Till date, I still marvel at the comments made by my father on the margins of virtually all the pages of Chairman Mao's **Essays on Military Warfare** which he had with him every day of the war, and which I read (the Essays and the comments) – during my high school days; comments which demonstrated the great parallels between the conditions of the struggle of the Chinese Communists and the Biafran resistance fighters, but a wide divergence between the brilliant Chinese communist responses and the inept and ill-conceived strategies of the Biafran commanding officers.

As we settled in our rural environment amidst the ruins of war, shattered hopes and broken homes and dreams, and in a 12-bedroom house whose lower floor was carpeted by dried excreta left behind by departing soldiers, and whose library had been used as screwed up tissue papers, it did occur to me that my earliest artistic impressions and, probably, the first formative ingredients of my creativity were deeply rooted in those special nights at Utu, near Nnewi, in both moon-laden and star-lit nights, and other nights of forbidden gloom and threatening thunder, as my father's BOFF comrades foregathered, drinking gin and singing songs of war, bravery and heroism. My love for poetry, drama and storytelling must have been formed then, as a 5 or 6 year-old, and till date I can still recite all those Biafran war songs which I memorized at heart and many of which were later celebrated by Chukwuemeka Ike in **Sunset at Dawn.**

Every family is a unique creation and has a unique identity. It expresses itself as a life force in a special manner with sets of communicable ethos, values and ideals never to be found exactly in other households.

For me, the peculiar, unique expression of our family identity lay in the effortless ease with which communication was carried out and shared, with candour, passion and contestation of ideas at every turn. Both my parents are totally liberal in their understanding of family relations and child upbringing. Even as elementary school pupils, our voices were to be heard loud and clear, from the upper floor to the main road just across the way, as we engaged our parents in impassioned discussions about life and reality. Friends and neighbours would always marvel at and comment about the "strange behaviour" of the Udentas who never seemed to cease talking and maybe arguing or disputing with one another.

Yet, a great spectacle awaited them at the sense of love, family devotion, loyalty, bond and commitment, and the near fierce and fanatical hero-worshipping by children of their parents. For in spite of our being bold at the discussion table, especially as we grew older and matured – a situation that almost always produced six varied points of view – we saw in them the reflection of God on earth and obeyed, respected and honoured them as good children were wont to.

This liberal parental disposition encouraged the flowering of personal potentials and self-expression, an attitude that we took to the extreme, sometimes, but now happily with no serious negative consequences. The oldest of us children, Fidelia, entered high school when the rest of us boys were still in elementary school, and during holidays, our sister being very sociable, extroverted and lively, our home became one of the social meeting centres and points of interaction for college boys, with music, dance, drinks and cigarettes in the mix. Music was supplied by my father's old gramophone player, whose sound production my immediate elder brother, Ben Jr., ingenuously increased by placing the speakers atop a large earthenware pot so as to produce the then popular resounding bass overlay.

Social parties, then called "pop", were to be held in our house or in some other liberal households, with the 45 rpm discs supplied, believe it or not, by our mother, whose fortnightly trips to Enugu to purchase drugs and other medical supplies for her maternity, also included the purchase of "pop" music carefully written down by my sister and eldest brother, Okey Maurice, with a charge that she should not come back unless all the discs in the list were bought!

Our music experience was formed by the burgeoning post-war pop music culture spawned by such creative geniuses and artistes as Jonathan Udensi (Spud Nathans), Manfred Best and Jerry Boifriand of the **Wings** (The group later split into two with the tragic death of Spud Nathans – arguably the best pop vocalist in the history of Nigerian pop music – with Best leading the **Original Wings** and Jerry Boifrand leading the **Super Wings**); Chyke Fusion and **The Apostles; Founder's 15; Black children; One World; Cloud 7;** Tony Grey; **Semi-colon;** Sunny Okosuns; Bongos Ikwue; **Blo**; Lijadu Sisters; and Ofege. Later, **Sweet Breeze** (some of whose leading members were my sister's schoolmates at IMT, Enugu); Chris Okotie; Jide Obi; and Christy Essien-Igbokwe were to become an intergral part of this rich musical and cultural exposure and experience. On the traditional side were **The Oriental Brothers,** Osadebe and the Peacocks International Band.

On reflection, I can justifiably say that our family environment and culture, our parents' liberalism, tolerance and understanding, and their expectation that we will and must eventually find our way and purpose in life made us live our life to the full, sometimes, in excess of social pursuits, far ahead of our age. On balance, it is to their greater glory and honour that we turned out right, and more than repaid their confidence in us.

My eldest sister, Fidelia Nkire, is married to Hon. Sam Nkire, a one-time commissioner in Abia State, a presidential ambassadorial nominee, a former member of a major federal board and presently the national chairman of one of Nigeria's leading political parties, the Progressive People's Alliance. Of their four children, the eldest, Queenette is presently pursuing her Masters degree in London. My eldest brother, Okey Maurice, is an accomplished and successful businessman who lives with his wife, Irene, and three daughters in Enugu. My immediate elder brother, Ben Junior, not long ago relocated to Abuja with his wife and three sons from their base at Abingdom, Maryland, USA.

As for me, the last born, I can equally claim a measure of self-attainment; having left university teaching as a Senior Lecturer; being a leading figure in the pro-democracy movement that resisted the late General Sani Abacha's tyranny; having served as the founding National Secretary of Alliance for Democracy, AD; and was until Dec. 2009 a Director in a Presidential Peace Building Institute.

I have gone into this relatively detailed account about how we, the children, turned out for, often times, I do reflect on what the situation could or may have been given the liberalism of our parents, their tolerance and even open, joyful acceptance of our vision of life and our place in it, and the unconditional allowance they gave us in choosing our careers and life partners. It was a balancing act that was successfully negotiated, and I strongly believe that if they had not attained the height they did, where upon we drew our inspiration, drive and motivation, maybe, that act would not have been well balanced.

However, let me quickly add that I can now, in retrospect, see something of their social strategy. While our parents were liberal in intellectual matters and social situations that connect us to others, they were strict disciplinarians in matters domestic. Our father may not speak out for months on end; his very commanding and influential presence was enough condition for order to reign. If it did get out of hand, as was the case usually with boys, and a boisterous girl of the ages of 8 -12, a smack or two from his cane would cause peace to reign for weeks on end.

Our mother, on the other hand, as most mothers are often given to perform, always had her hand to aid her tongue as she instilled family discipline and compliance to family tasks and responsibilities of orderliness, hardwork, diligence and obedience virtually on hourly basis. It may be correct to stress that the combination of social and intellectual liberalism and permissiveness with strict enforcement of discipline and good conduct at the home front, in domestic situations, may be the objective force that helped in tilting the scale in favour of the relative success we have all made of our lives.

My first recollection of school was a low, mud walled, thatched-roof, rectangular building that leaked very badly when it rained. The door way was always wet, soggy and damp. The open space in front of the building always ran with sluggish water and debris, especially along the gutters. I could also picture millipedes squirming in and out of the soggy earth. For one reason or the other my mind was never fully given to the words of the teacher or the activities inside the "classroom", but was always constantly centred on the wet earth around me, the squirming millipedes, in blind, terror-ridden fascination. While it always seemed to rain in my recollection, I cannot say. This was at Utu, probably, around mid-1969.

When my family eventually settled at our ancestral village of Mgbowo in 1970, my "classroom" was only slightly better. I started Elementary One again, under a huge mango tree that dominated the entrance to Central School Mgbowo, with its gnarled, exposed roots serving as our seats. But schooling in the village was a beautiful experience. Recitations of verses were a regular occurrence during the morning assembly, and so also were the numerous singing lessons that heralded the end of a school year or the graduation of Elementary Six pupils. I enjoyed those singing sessions and the learning of alphabets, rendered in a song-like fashion. I enjoyed also the sense of illumination and expansion of the imagination engendered by a particularly inspired social studies teacher whose name I have forgotten but who we all collectively owed our knowledge of the world and current affairs as he spoke eloquently yet under another mango tree that he preferred to instruct us probably in our elementary four or five.

The choice of this tree was deliberate by him, for by then the classrooms had been equipped with desks and chairs, yet he preferred to fire our youthful imagination outside the confines of a classroom block, insisting instead that we commune with nature outside. I guess my love for nature, of plants, trees and animals, and my passion for politics and world affairs were formed then.

Our after school experiences, especially during long vacations, exemplified the poetry of living in a rural environment. We hunted rats, lizards, bush rabbits, and grass cutters, set traps for crabs in muddy patches leading to the village streams, and for birds that ate up the maize in the farm. We swam inside the muddy waters of the streams and fished with anything we could lay hands on, sometimes, with such a deadly chemical as gamalin 20, the purchase of which I had the honour or dishonour of undertaking, being the last born and the most innocent-looking. We picked wild berries, 'Icheku', locusts and the lava or pupa of butterflies that infested the village breadfruit trees.

Opportunities to read abounded in our house. My father gradually rebuilt his library and began subscribing to **Awake**, the Jehovah Witnesses publication; a venture that ultimately produced over 30 bound volumes in the 1980s and 1990s. Till date my love for **Awake** never abated, and I still acquire the odd copy or two, every now and then. I cannot now fully recollect all that I read from my father's fairly large stock of books, but as I gradually grew older and entered high school, I did recall that between classes two or three and five, I had read, several times over, Will Durant's **The Story of Philosophy,** and **The History of Political Thought** (the author of who I cannot recollect, and a book my father, on a particular occasion, took away from me, pointing out that it was far too mature for my age).

That must have been in my class three or four. I also formed my first impressions about Marxism and communism by reading a short, introductory series published by Western scholars, and dealing with a critique of Lenin's positions on several subjects: ***Lenin and Imperialism, Lenin on the State and Revolution, Lenin and the National Question,*** etc. I also read from his rich stock of English and American poetry books, and his own writings.

Being a boarding student in a village secondary school (I attended Awgu County Secondary School, later renamed Awgu High School, Nenwe, Awgu L.G.A. in Enugu State, which was established in 1958 when county colleges flourished, and which must have had its high points in the 1960s before the war, but which suffered the fate many a school in Eastern Nigeria suffered after the war: decay of infrastructure, poor funding, poor staffing, etc), which was a mere 3 kilometres from my village of Mgbowo, afforded me some opportunities for intellectual growth and the nursing of the creative spirit.

We had a crop of teachers (my father had just left the school in 1975 as I was entering it to take up a post as an Education Officer in the local government headquarters), who were dedicated, who knew their stuff and who were prepared to go the extra mile, limited facilities notwithstanding, to impart as much knowledge on us as they possibly could.

My love for books and reading, which was already deeply entrenched during my elementary school days, grew stronger when I entered secondary school. I recollect being appointed the Librarian of class 1C, my class, or probably the librarian of the whole class, and finding myself spending long hours soaking up as much as I could in the serene environment of the school library. I read virtually the whole works of Enid Blyton, particularly ***The Famous Five*** series. I read the poetry of Lord Alfred Tennysson, Matthew Arnold, Lord Byron, Alexander Pope, and the American Transcendentalists. I also read Caryle's ***Classical Myths, Myths and Legends of Ancient Greece, Classical Myths in Song and Story,*** and different versions of Homer's ***Iliad*** and ***The Odyssey.***

I can also recall that I read a particular volume of **The Encyclopedia Britannica** which I enjoyed but found very difficult to understand, the works of Shakespeare (the drama texts, his sonnets and the stories derived from the drama texts), and some African novels. My hometown being only 40 kilometres from Enugu, I found myself making weekly journeys to purchase novels and other creative works under the African writers series edition (I did pride myself that I read virtually all the works in the series in print and available in book stores in Enugu before I left high school), and such socialist publications as **New Dawn, Socialism: Theory and Practice** and **Socialism: Principles, Practice and Prospects.** I also bought and read all the novels of James Hadley Chase and Nick Carter available in Enugu (indeed my nickname as a high school student was Kill Master: Nick Carter's secret service rating no, and a name that my high school mates and friends still call me till this date). I also bought and read all the writings of Tuesday Lobsang Rampa, including his most definitive work, **I Believe**, apart from **The Third Eye, Doctor from Lhasa,** etc. All these were in addition to buying and reading virtually all the novels and stories in the Pacesetter series and Mills and Boon series, and also as many novels of Barbara Cartland, Denise Robbins and Harold Robbins that I could lay my hands on.

My youthful imagination and creative desire were also fired by such prescribed reading texts in classes one and two in high school; Chinua Achebe's **Chike and the River,** Cyprian Ekwensi's **The Drummer Boy, An African Night's Entertainment** and **The Passport of Mallam Illia** (I read **Burning Grass** which I found difficult and hard-going, **Jagua Nana** and **People of the City** on my own); Onuora Nzekwu and Michael Crowther's **Eze Goes to School** (the most popular and influential of the prescribed texts); **Trouble in Form Five; One Week, One Trouble; The Adventures of Souza;** Anezi Okoro's **New Broom at Amanzu** and **The Village Headmaster,** and very many others.

The list of the African novels in the African Writers Series that left indelible mark in my mind and helped to germinate any creative impulses in my class two-four include: Chinua Achebe's

Things Fall Apart, *No Longer at Ease*, *Arrow of God* and *A Man of the people;* Wole Soyinka's ***The Interpreters*** (which I found very difficult); Amu Djoleto's ***The Strange Man***; Stanlake Samkange's ***On Trial For My Country;*** and Kenneth Kaunda's ***Zambia Shall Be Free*** (probably the most popular African autobiography among the students, with the possible exception of Achebe's ***Things Fall Apart).*** Ngugi wa Thiong'o's ***Weep Not Child*** was hugely popular among students, so also his **The River Between** and *A Grain of Wheat.* The same could be said of John Munonye's ***The Only Son*** and ***Obi*** (I was to read his ***A Bridge to a Wedding*** and **The Oil Man of Obange** as a student of English and Literary Studies at the University of Nigeria, Nsukka); Onuora Nzekwu's **My Mercedes is Bigger Than Yours**; Obi B. Egbuna's ***Diary of a Homeless Prodigal*** (which inspired one of the texts in this volume), ***Elina*** and ***The Madness of Didi;*** T.M. Aluko's ***One Man, One Wife*** (another very popular novel with students) and ***One Man, One Machete.*** (I was eventually to read virtually all his other novels as a university student, including **His Worshipful Majesty** and **Chief The Honourable Minister);** and Chukwuemeka Ike's **Sunset at Dawn** and **The Potter's Wheel** which made a great impression on me as a high school student. I was to eventually read his **The Naked Gods, Toads for Supper, The Chicken Chasers, Expo '77** and his other novels as a university student.

These are some of the novels, stories, drama works, etc that I still recollect having read in high school. I not only read them, but bought them. However, as was usually the case, I eventually lost most of them; though I have made tremendous effort to re-stock my library with all these books and more. The list of the materials I read was surely far longer than the listing above, but I have captured some of them as a way of demonstrating the sources of my creative vision and the way and manner that my imagination was fired. Readers of these volumes will see, note and observe that some of my boyhood works were influenced by some of these books, and that echoes of them, direct and, sometimes, very dangerous, abound in the volumes.

Yet, in spite of what one can call the preparation of the mind

I was a very bad student in my classes one and two. At the end of each term, and during promotion examinations, I always found myself toward the tail end of the class. The reason may have been the distraction caused by my absorption with extra-curricular reading materials, but also being the last born, with two older brothers who were in the same school, I must have felt over-sheltered and over-protected that it took me sometime before I could find my independent feet and allow my natural endowments and talents to flower and flourish.

I became a better student in my class three, and may have been the best student during the promotion examinations from class four to class five, a feat that earned me the honour of being appointed a study prefect for class one and two students, and the whole school librarian. By the end of my class four I had read the WASC syllabus maybe three or four times over and, to all intents and purposes, was fully ready then for the WASC and JAMB examinations. Indeed, I took the JAMB examination in the second term of form five and was the second candidate admitted to read English at UNN. It was while already in the university that the WASC results came out, confirming my status as a university student.

And in full consultation with a number of my school mates, my brother Ben Jr., Austine Okeke, Charles Okeke, Emmanuel Akpa, the late Chris Aju, Anayo Simon Agu (who was the school senior prefect) and Patrick Isiogwu, I virtually stopped attending classes for the whole of Form Five, declaring in my youthful exuberance that those who really desire knowledge already have it; the passing of English, Chemistry and Physics, etc being not dependent on Grieve and Pratt, Lambert and Nelkon, etc respectively!

Interestingly, I did extremely well in the WASC mock examinations (I recollect scoring A1 in about 7 or 8 subjects, and together with Aju and Patrick Isiogwu, defied our history teacher's belief that no student will score A1 in his mock examination, by all scoring A1 + in same). Virtually all my closest schoolmates passed the main WASC examinations with either a Division 1 or a good Division 2 level of pass.

I suspect that I began writing in earnest about the beginning of 1977 when I was in form two. I wrote consistently during the next two years or so, after school hours, late at night in various school classrooms, and especially during long vacations. In retrospect, I do believe that I may have enjoyed reading and writing to other social activities, including dancing, dating and hanging out with friends, but all these I did and enjoyed enormously, though on each occasion I would usually come back to continue from where I stopped.

My most productive creative years were 1977-1979. I do not think that I wrote much in 1980, the year I graduated from high school. I was, however, not alone in this creative pursuit. Who started it may never be known, but a fledging creative writing tradition was spawned among a few of us which led to a healthy rivalry and a positive spirit of competition and the search for excellence. Somehow or the other, the news filtered out that I was writing novels, drama sketches and such like. When I eventually let in my close friends what I was up to, read my writings to them and pasted same on a weekly basis, on the wall beside my corner at Akanu Ibiam Hostel, yet another story began making the rounds that our school senior prefect, Anayo Agu who is now with the American Embassy in Lagos but who we all called Asasi Agu, was also into something very special.

It was soon discovered that he had conceived a mythopoeic interpretation of the essence of the mysterious water-maid with creative derivatives from "Omo" stream, a small, slow moving stream that bounded our school. He was to be seen at the bank of this stream, probably drawing inspiration from its inscrutable depths. Eventually, he came out with his prose-poetry work, called "Omodima," a creative piece that was peerless at the time.

While I may have been the most versatile and prolific in the range of genres I covered in my writings I was by no means the only writer around, and probably not even the best in terms of the maturity of vision and structure of presentation. Apart from Asasi Agu, the following classmates of mine also tried their hands in creative writing. My immediate elder brother, Ben Jr. wrote a beautiful novelette set in our village, maybe in response to the challenge set by my writings, which may have become a nuisance to him. The spirit of "I can do better than you" must have stimulated his creative consciousness and nudged his imaginative spirit for he, indeed, did craft an elegant work that none of mine ever dusted. The search for that manuscript continues and if seen, I do hope to convince him, Asasi Agu and the rest of them (if they can still find their manuscripts), to put out a companion volume to this series.

Engr. Emmanuel Akpa who works with PHCN, in Enugu also tried his hand in creative writing and editorial work. So did Patrick Isiogwu and the late Chris Aju, and maybe a few others whose names I cannot presently remember. It was, of course, not surprising that, with the exception of Emma Akpa, the rest of us were arts-based or inclined, and it was then something special for him, a science student, to hold his own very much in our midst. It was, again, not by accident that we all belonged to the debating society and represented the school at local, zonal and state-wide debating and quiz competitions.

The spirit of dialogue, debate, discourse, competition and friendly rivalry pervaded our academic and social space and urged us to greater heights of endeavour. It was principally this spirit, cast in a provincial, rural clime, but hot and passionate, in combination with the more pristine currents and forces that shaped my life and conditioned my personality and identity, that led to the creation of the works that I will be shortly introducing.

The works collected in these volumes are by no means the only ones I wrote when I was in high school. There are two others I can still remember but which are yet to be seen or discovered. One was a novel based in South Africa and dealt with the psychological trauma of a child growing up in the then apartheid enclave. It must have been inspired by my role as Ndaba in Tunji Fatilewa's play, **Torrents of Soweto**, a performance we put together for the School's Founder's Day Celebration. That must have been around November-December 1979, at the beginning of the first term of my form five. The second was a novelette based in an urban environment, the subject matter of which I cannot recollect, but I could still feel the images of my father, my mother, myself, my siblings and close friends in my consciousness of the text as I put these thoughts down.

One other comment worth making here is that as I tried to re-read all the works, one or two things stand out. Most of them were, alas badly or poorly written (a point I have already made) and reflected my immaturity in written English.

Secondly, because I read so much, I virtually forced out my ill-absorption of most of the works in my own creative productions.

Precisely because I wanted to command the use of English very powerfully and write as the masters of the language wrote, I used expressions anyhow, and on numerous occasions even invented my own words that apparently meant nothing! Readers of these volumes will see this difficult search by a yet to be fully formed mind that sought gallantly but sometimes vainly to create something out of his very fertile imagination and consciousness.

Again, because I will be making very short comments in the 'Author's Note' to each of the volumes, what is now left for me to do is to present their organizational and contentual structure. The six volumes which are presented below are:

1. Volume One
   i. **The Wrath of the Gods** – a novel

2. Volume Two
   i. **Book of Knowledge and Great Understanding** – extracts from several works, and original philosophical musings and social commentary
   ii. **Reflections on School Life** – an account of different aspects of secondary school life

3. Volume Three
   i. **Before They Came** – a novel

4. Volume Four
   i. **Poetic Reminiscences** – a collection of poems
   ii. **Book of Dislocation** – a collection of poems
   iii. **Lyrics and other Traditional Longer poems** – collection of poems.

5. Volume Five
    i. ***The Re-discovery of the Arlistoga*** – a detective/thriller novel
    ii. ***Retrospective Vision: Cultural Interactions*** – a collection of short stories
6. Volume Six
    i. **The Quarrel** (A Play)
    ii. **Chief Eze Isiagu's Troubles** (A Short Story)
    iii. **The Air Raid** (A Short Story)
    iv. **The Return of the People** (A Short Story)
    v. **Personality Clash in Hades** – part of a poetic drama
    vi. **Some Stories Told** – collection of short stories

The above titles were the original ones I gave to the works, with the exception of the explanation separated by a dash. The titles are retained as I gave them when the works were written, even though why some of them were so titled, and what symbolism I had in mind, is anybody's guess.

Finally, it is my hope and expectation that even though these works may not mean much to present-day mature, or even young readers, they were a part of my growing up and artistic and intellectual development, and a part of my history that I don't want lost. This is my modest defense in putting these volumes out; a defense that may appear weak to some, but which, nevertheless, points to a certain poignant, though grossly imperfect beginning, in consideration of the totality of my later intellectual productions.

Udenta O. Udenta
Abuja
February, 2014

I

Book of Knowledge and Great Understanding

Lesson One
What a Writer Will Do

i. A writer will spend his time and days combining the ever-enquiring mind and near-masochist dare-devilry of a child, the painful loneliness and invigilated veracity, the unsoiled and expensive indifference to material poverty. The near death wish flouting of authority and selfish craving for immortality, the insatiable lust for questions and answers, the spoilt – brat yearnings for the attention of humanity and the shock absorption potentiality that often shape, de-shape and misshape her destiny. —Obi B. Egbuna.

ii. The Face Value of A good Writer's Book, The Constructions and His Command of English:
The qualities of a good writer. His books should possess such recommendations, for instance its mellifluous prose poetry, its brutal frankness, and agonizing realism. The author's command of English language blends beautifully with the lack of squeamishness even in matters which conventional society would like to dress up in euphemistic gloss.
For example, when one wants to describe the celebration of the beauty of womanhood, and alludes tantalizingly to the "misty" duskiness of dreamland and time or when one plots the tangents of sorrow that can grow out of war and vents the spleen on the human vampire, who seek the blood of his fellow men in the name of technological superiority. If you think the white liberal is a better friend of the black man than a confused fascist maniac like John Voster, our black power evangelist knows better for the only difference

between them is that of tactics, not of principle. Their quarrel is only between frankness and hypocrisy within a fascist framework." —Obi B. Egbuna

It requires a talented artist to write a credible letter to an unborn baby or to see through the distortions, mental, physical, of a modern Nigerian bluestocking whose "carcass of creamy fiction which has been whittled away by self imposed tyranny of postcolonial decadence evokes so much pity and horror." —Obi B. Egbuna

iii. **Philosophical State of Man**

Our life is a shadow; a merz perfume which waits upon the sun to reduce. Vain, therefore, is the ambition of man who seeks by trophies and dead things to leave a living name behind. He only weaves but nets to catch the wind! ***AND THIS IS CRASS STUPIDITY!***

iiib **Laxity and Salvation Among Men**

Comrades, no lingering behind, the time wasted is the time lost, the period saved is the time gained. The nature of affairs nowadays is like a rhythmical, beautiful dance that vibrates and sends a cold shiver down everybody's spine, like the formidable, fantastic and supernatural power of great Poseidon's ocean waves. It looks awful, stars gone, the sun shines dully and the pregnant moon appears and reappears among the gloomy and cloudy, shadowy sky.

Comrades, what are we waiting for? Backward never, forward ever. The fruitful gain of this world surpasses the extravagance and material opulence of a multi-millionaire. The great success lies in the secret of survival. Health is wealth my colleagues. Time is running short, the sun is burning hard, and the rain is beating and pouring down in hot torrents.

Causes of failure in human objectives and ambition will be summed up as moral laxity. Corruptive lives have injected a snail-like speed growth of useful activities in the nerves of young men, and they are succumbing and sprawling like a fallen boxer into Shoal. The way to their doom is at hand, the wisdom of truth vanished into the thin air.

At this crucial and critical time, the roaming of thieves, smugglers and evil men of underworld, the pocket searchers and all other unwarranted ways of activities that pain like a pin stuck in the eyes of old men and elders as they tumble over things and sigh sorrowfully, remembering their youthful days.

iiic. Negative Attitude and Likely Repercussions

The proportional change in the life of mortals can never be altered. It sticks like a flowing blood that spilt along the steep alley. The nature of truth could not be reached, when the harp rose high, the lyre boomed now, the cymbals sounded, well, the earth will shake and men will be lost in dreamland. Useful attention forgotten? Yes! A thousand times yes!

What do you, then, think the creator will do? Keep dormant? No! Alas! Wait, the repercussion is obligated to happen and the final purification and cleansing rites done will be tremendous. Then, men may know that the Almighty is a saving and a destroying God for in Luke it states that, "Jesus will cause the rise and fall of many in Israel". Another evocative verse in the gospel is where Jesus said that he will cause to be that 'father will be fighting against son, daughter against mother, mother -in-law against daughter-in-law and father-in-law against son-in-law".

How disastrous it will be. The philosophers can't tell you, but an estimated consequence of each disaster surpasses Job's suffering. What a time! What a trouble! What a sin!

Lesson Two

i. **Be a Thinking Man**

Has it not ripened yet; if so why the extraordinary predictions? But it looks and seems to me as if it is moving sideways as a crab moves; why not think, be like the Old Greek thinkers and possess the golden qualities of the old philosophers. Accept and let your moves and motivations be crowned by the immortal praises of the inventive geniuses. Dullness and idleness are the greatest setback in human powers. The problem of manpower strikes like a ten-year drought but overpopulation is pestering us. Good for nothing, yes! It may be so! As darkness darkens, the maturation is inevitable. Strive hard for success is yours.

Why do you like to remain asleep and keep dormant? If it goes on like this nothing superb would be invented. This is why human knowledge must be applied to make the salvation of objects possible. As it looks, and the gaze slight, the weakness is exposed as the blackness of Satan, and heard like the eerie hooting of the owl that bellowed and pierced like the sharp edge of metal gong's "diminuendo'. Cover it quick and close your eyes in shameful mistakes. Try harder and win fame. "A popular man is good but a famous man thinks better and commands more respect." The mind is plagued, and the retribution is fierce and noticeable. It is amorous, it is incredible, it is incredulous. Have we been brainwashed? Possibly no! Why, then, do misadventure reign, and if not, is it predictable? Why are we unnerved? Why are we puzzled about life? No! A million times no! Don't be fearful but keep calm and think things over and see the great answer and wonderful desire pulsing inside your memory.

ii. Think Hard and Achieve Much. Imitation is Suicide

My friends, words of wisdom is the greatest teacher of all time, and the knowledge of philosophy is the best achievement a man has ever attained since he was born. As the span of his days runs short, he leans on his walking stick and pours out words of understanding to his younger people. Why do you behave intoxicatingly, and in a tipsy state? Insanity and human power is disastrous and unreasoning is dangerous. The brutal clash between men and the agonizing nature of human beings is the reciprocal advantage of evil force. The day is running short and nothing is achieved. Why do you stay idle? What are you waiting for? There was a metallic laughter and the monotonous savage roar of rising waves as the days ran further away.

How could it be solved? As I said before, think hard and understand much. Imitation is suicide. Why is your enquiring minds low? Why do you keep your eyes shut and gaze ,moppingly along the breezy nature, waiting for manna to fall from heaven? The cry of sorrow is hoarse and the salvation among men poor! Marauding savages and wild creatures we have turned out to be, delighting ourselves in the spilling and shedding of human blood, but the inventiveness of the mind is small.

The huge space of human brain is occupied by ways to waggle at treasures and be the richest man alive. Is that what will solve perplexing human problems? No! A hundred times capital No! In fact, things are moving upside down and the way to get out is narrow. Strive hard and let success crown your aim for the names of great thinkers and philosophers is like a crocodile's faeces, if you want to clean it, it cannot go. Why not be like them! Material wealth, I agree, is worth possessing but does it send away the unhappiness and problems facing man now, economically, physically, mentally, politically and scientifically? It is left for you to decide.

What is hindering the mind of mortals, diverting their attention from inventive and productive reasoning? If this be all the condition of all living things may the day be cursed when it started and the night that said it. A living creature is produced, so may the stars of the sky be thin and the moon dull and moody. May the dawn be long, wanting light but finding none. May the day he put the potion that intrigues human brain be counted out from the days of the year and evil wishes be his possession. If men themselves are consumed by crass stupidity, let them be wiped out but, let the eye of men be open to know that which is good and that which, if taken, will lead to doom.

"Don't be impromptu! Don't be unexpectant! Don't be abashed! Never be amazed! Don't be surprised! And astonished! Think hard, and surely you will be rich in know ledge surpassing material wealth. Your fame will defy death and be immortal! Help yourself!

iii. Use Your Initiative and Think Well

The indelibleness of failure in human objectives is shocking. The reputation of man will not be regarded satisfactorily if he is not fully successful in all his motives and endeavours. Frustration and willful confrontation will not be solved if thinking is not applied. The world is like a legendary mist where the presence of the ageless monster is felt. Lazy men will be thrown into unquenchable fire where the lake is burning day and night, but the hard working, thinking men, solving the nation's unsur mountable problems will enjoy everlasting joy. Don't be stunned! Don't be dizzy! Don't be dazed, and never be subtle, but face them with the available resources and your initiative, success will be yours.

iv. Boycott Evil Ways and Be Happy

Why should it be allowed? The right measures to be taken

will be like a dawning moon that chases insanity away. It supports the traditional livelihood, local culture and communal rituals. Think deep, ladies and gentlemen, and boycott the strange intoxicating activities that nearly pushed us into a serious dilemma. FESTAC! Yes, it was the greatest measure and a good step among black powers in the twentieth century. "Black is beautiful, black is stainless, black is supernatural." He who is not proud of his colour will not be fit to live. Don't be ecstatic and don't be vulnerable. Brushing aside iniquities will be encouraged but don't be over enthusiastic. Maddened zealotry should be forgotten, so that you can think deep before taking any action. The Racist, Fascist, Apartheid inequality of mankind propagated by the maniac Ian Smith and his brutal, vandalistic and barbaric collaborators will be stopped. What benefit are they serving us? Habouring him! No! Fight hard, sacrifice yourself and free our brothers from the yoke of colonization, neo-colonization and imperialism. Do well, brothers, and rejoice like the animals in the Manor Farm when the tyrannic, despotic, autocratic and lunatic Jones was expelled for ever.

All humanity must be liberated. Think well and know the problems confronting us. Try hard and reason deep, and see yourself in a new state of affairs. Mbonu Ojike! Yes, the bold man! Thanks to him! Immortal fame he has! Why not think well and do like him. Develop your own philosophy and act independently, but visit a wise man and learn from him. You will be wiser yet. Read deep and understand life. Philosophize your knowledge but act wisely.

ॐ | *Lesson Three* | ॐ
"Who Owns The World?"

Don't Be Obstinate and Never Feel UNfit At All

Why are you proud? Vomitting evil wordings, superbly dishing out atrocities with impunity. Dance backwards and forward, the vacant opening of human problem and chronic difficulty shine like the terrible rays of light from a mad sun. Are all problems solved, and are you feeling self-satisfied? No! My brothers, millionaire or not, the debt you owe the world must be paid. Don't laugh because the full claim on you will come and deeds of immorality will bear disastrous consequences. The world is for whom? Ha! Ha! Ha! Such was the ogenic laughter of intelligent philosophers as foolish creatures roam about, murmuring and muttering words such as "the world is ours" or "the world is for us."

Sit down on a three legged, old, archaic stool, bend your head, your hand placed on your jaw, think deep and see if the truth will be far from being reached. Leave material wealth and don't be a pleasure-seeker which is the easiest way to human failure, and the open and wide channel to your doom. Life is like a possessed spirit which chases sanity away and reigns with maniacal power until the full treasure trove is taken, the inheritor banished and pleasant atmosphere created. Don't be stubborn and obstinate, and think well before saying anything.

No man is fit on earth. A man who thinks he is fit for anything is like a hallowed *Ikoro* which booms and rends the air with its unsurpassed message. Outwardly it seems big and gigantic; inwardly, an empty wood making much noise. Such is any man abusing the name of nature. He is like a broken bottle which cannot be mended. The stupidity and folly among men is troubling. Don't think you are rich; stay cool and think wisely. See, now, all your encroaching problems will be solved and, with naked eyes, you will see them dissolving like an ice block, and vanishing into thin air like an exposed vapour.

35

❧| *Lesson Four* |❧

Social Evils and Corruptive Lives Reigning Instead?

"Think and Banish the Deadly Vituperations"

It was first rumoured but established itself like a wonderful truth but many allowed themselves to be caught in the entangling webs of social evils. As long as it seems movable the day came when all devilish and satanic activities were like-wise banished in a prolific way. The vibrating, intense sun had almost completed its day's journey, and very soon impenetrable blanket of ebony cloud awaited the earth. That's when they want to strike and accomplish their evil aims. Why? The intoxicating heat of the work full day was twitching and cooling off; when the clanging, irritating noise and busy activities of the city, both legal and illegal, were dwindling; and when the brightness of the sun has been engulfed by darkness- that was the time marauders set about their work.

What! Moving upside down? Yes, the full enjoyment of city life, the opulence of luxury living, absent minded fools who don't think twice and who make good citizenship the object of caricature. Here goes he, who has been dislocated because of his work, good virtues and thinking knowledge, his inability and lack of inclination to engage in perilous ventures, his total lack of dynamism and his appalling slowness to cope with the fast, almost insanely – intoxicating taste of their ruinous society.

In short, evil ambitious aspiration and opportunism are weapons used against peace-loving citizens who are utterly dissatisfied with the state of existence and who become their objects of vituperations.

When will you see and change fast? Again, as another verse

indicates, their syncretism with regard to law and order is still engulfed by thick smoky mist. They are still visionless and sightless, polluting nature, marshalling, fishing for and grabbing wealth from all possible channels and avenues, for no conceivable reason. The flamboyant show-off of the rich with their greedily accumulated wealth and corruptive lives breed laxity in social development. All these have injected a complex power intrigue among the wealthy with their craving for immediate satisfaction; a situation that has chained them to the bottom of the world, the real, thinking world.

Why? Can't patience be exerted? To get wealth means to sweat your brow. Don't do it the easy way, but settle down and think well before acting, or profoundly embarrassing ruin will overwhelm you, and push you into succumbing and sprawling among the tiny nymphs of great oceanic sea. Patience! Sweat! Work! Think! Fill your retentive memory with rich thought!

II
"Deep Thinking Solves Your Reptilous Foolishness"

> What hearkens, cries, strikes deep, purified by change, damning the messy open-cut life and altering mankind with necessary change. Think! World-wide awakening! Splash! The singing of sorrowful song scatters the mind of the bounded and heart-broken. It was not so obvious at first, but I laughed along the sloppy, steep bank of immortal river, jesting and disdainfully, eyeing the damaged route of creative work.
>
> It came in cadences of upward emotions, supporting trembling knowledge.

Bribery and corruption, black business, intrigues, blackmail, rancour, and witch-hunting characterize the life of the unpleasant dwellers of envious social world. What holds you from stepping into the clean footpath of those inventive geniuses? The knowledge of men nowadays has no root given their social evils:

cheating and corruptive lives, especially among our city dwellers which have not been banned.

Solution-thinking, knowledge and man's ability to see good from bad, and avoid iniquitous values.

> The vibrating and violently shaking laughter moves the rhythmical silence. While it sounded, what can reptiles and mammalians reproduce? Contrast it with the old, ageless passage of time till the dawn of goodness crept out.

Listen well and see what I have said. It all boils down to isolated activities much wanted to aid the wheel of life. We have two large eyes, yet we cannot see. We have ears, but can't hear, two nostrils but never can detect and separate evil from good. Our mouth is wide open, gulping down all that enters its way both legal and illegal. Question yourself and feel safe, shaming all devices to vanish with tremendous force.

While plunging humanity into endless suffering in the name of chasing wealth, the treasure cove of mortal value succumbs when full fledged joy of deathless origin appears. Solution – well trained thinking and knowledge of philosophy will help you, especially "in case of incasity." What more can I say? Just think, think, think!

✣| *Lesson Five* |✤

Fake and False Pledges and Ethnic Problem

See the gluttony and war consciousness of some people, who are dancing forward and backward, along the corridor, not minding the general public and the suffering of their fellow humans. The most regrettable part is the encroaching politics of instability, unpredictability, volatility, corruption, vindictiveness and uncertainty.

What drives high ambition can be summarized thus – those at the top make vain, "undoable", hopeless and almost unheard of pledges which arouse hopes and aspirations but their unfulfilment boils down to frustration which finds outlets in violence, riots, public demonstration and other fissiparous tendencies.

The unification principle, if lacked by the operators of any government, will see a state of chaos, perennial ethnic chauvinism, and where jingoistic tribal affiliations have taken a deep root. The ruler will bear in mind that such unwanted divisions will turn the country people into a stubborn, obstinate, intractable and ungrateful people.

This small passage deals with two points; hopeless promises made by unreasoning rulers and their inability to treat ethnic problems and crush stubborn good-for-nothing jingoists. The second is the much craving for power that leads to instability and unpatriotic life in a country. A simple minded person will not think overnight and see what will be done so that tranquility, peace, goodwill, fair play and harmonious life will be patrolling and oiling the wheel of life. A good leader who studies his people will see to it that he consoles them about other encroaching and entangling problems and plead with them to exercise patience, but not to start to make empty and unwanted pledges that he will never accomplish.

Malignant and anarchic problems will face a country with ethnic and tribal affliction and jingoism if the leader is not iron-willed and without leadership acumen. It could be tribal wars, unrest of mind, rancour, intrigue and blackmail, with its people acting like those who are brainwashed, hypnotized, drugged and witch-hunted. Their mind will be poisoned. Yes! Their mind will surely be poisoned!

The only deliverance and salvation the people will have is their endurance, and the understanding that all the people of a country are brothers and sisters despite their historical backgrounds and origins, economic resources, religious worship, tribal languages, and the existing political nature. Without these things the country will never survive in this modern and jet age unless it wants to sprawl and join the bygone early, ape man age.

A typical oriental despot, like the puppet regime set up by the USA imperialism, is the sworn enemy of the Korean people. The tyrannical and dictatorial way of ruling never ensures success by those who have attempted it, those who are practising it, and those who will put it into show in future.

Instead, it leads to brutal clashes, often associated with coup d'état, producing agonizing, terrorizing and terrible result. Brutal atrocities, barbaric and vandalistic action will be the object of the day.

II
Irreligiousity Promotes and Propels Indiscipline and Insanity

The advancement in technology will never change the blanket of warped mentality of those uncharitable nations and individuals from plunging into and indulging in barbarism but the charity of the Almighty, moral understanding and deep thinking, with sweating brows, foster humanity. This makes us accept that we are all brothers despite our different nationalities. The physiological aspect of human objectives is slow but oppression, inequality and fascism in social development will never solve the recent problems encroaching all around the world.

The high rate of indiscipline in the society is alarming, almost in surmountable and unsubtle. What we have now are people of backbiting strata, haters of God, insolent and proud braggarts, violators of law of nature and humanity, and all other types of immoral living. When this continues what will the God living in heaven do? The creator will send famine, plaque, and pestilence, earthquake, war, inflation, and nuclear war. Revolting pride, lust and oppression will be what he will send to dwell among us as companions.

If any one follows the nature of this world it will impel us to violence, vandalistic act, wrong way of life and work, while religion and moral truth lead to meekness, humility, endurance, forbearance, charity, generosity, kindness and selflessness.

In short, the only powerful motive that can restrain the human mind from utter distraction is a force that is full of virtue that can tame the human mind, sensibility, passion, emotion and human aspiration.

2

Reflections on School Life

Chapter One
The Hunting Expedition

Hunting expeditions had not been in practice in secondary schools, but in our own case we just did it for experimental purposes. We, the most junior students, had not known anything nor had ever heard anything about 'Integrated Science', up till that moment. So, when we had stayed about four days since coming back to school after the term break, the Integrated Science master came to our class.

The first thing he taught us was about some animals and their habits. Although we did not understand it fully, he said that we must learn it from our notes and exercise books. He said that, to understand it fully, that we should go on a hunting expedition in search of some animals that we will make use of when we come back.

He gave us a fortnight to prepare ourselves fully well; we shall go with equipments for hunting, including machetes. He also advised us to carry things like bread and biscuits in case we became hungry. When the time was approaching, he went and got permission from the principal. The principal gave his consent. He also got permission, so that some tubers of yams should be given to him so that we will eat it when we felt hungry.

We were also advised to hold water bottles so that we can fill them with water which we will drink when we feel thirsty. Preparations were made thus; those who had no water bottle borrowed from others, those who had their canvas put it in order; and those who didn't have borrowed from those that had but were not going. This hunting expedition comprised all class one students, both boarders and day students, but some class two boys were allowed to go because they were offering Intergrated

Science also.

On the appointed day, everybody assembled in front of one big mango tree to wait for the master who was taking us in Inter-Science and who will lead the way. When he arrived later on, everybody stood up and we greeted him in the usual way. Little preparations were made on where to go and who knew the place that was good for hunting.

This question concerned mostly those who were natives of the nearest towns, like Nnewe, Mgbowo and Awgu. A volunteer from Nnewe came forward and said that he will lead us to the place that was best suitable for hunting. He went forward and we followed him behind. After walking for about forty yards, he led us into a thick bush which he knew best. When he entered he showed us the particular part that was good for hunting.

With this knowledge, we advanced into the place, taking our positions as we went. We formed a circle round the chosen bush. Some people took it as their work to make noise and beat the sticks they carried in their hands on the bush. After a short time, a grass cutter appeared. It was chased; it ran into the next bush. We pursued it to that place and continued running round and round with it until finally, a blow from the machete I was carrying in my hand killed it. It was taken and put into the bag which we were carrying and which was meant for that purpose. We continued hunting until we did not know when we went away from the bush we had been hunting before and went into a distant one. There, we caught a rat alive, according to the master's instruction not to kill it.

We did not know when we passed two miles on the expedition. On the second mile we killed many animals and caught many alive. When we reached a tree shade, we settled down to rest. There, those who had something ate it but the yams were not cooked because the master leading us said that it was when we had finished the expedition and were about to go home that we shall eat it. After the eating and resting, we resumed our journey.

On our way we saw an owl that was almost half dead. We picked it, and down it went into our bag. We encountered a giant rat and, soon, it was on the way to its safety. We pursued it. A boy dived at it, the beast opened its mouth to bite, the boy let go and soon it ran as fast as it could. We still kept on pursuing it until one boy unleashed a tremendous blow from the machete he was carrying, and deep it went into the poor brain of the ugly beast. A fire was made and it was roasted there and eaten.

When we finished that exercise we were again on the move. We soon passed Mgbowo town, but by then everybody was tired and hungry. Luckily for us we saw two mango trees full of mangoes that were ripe, together with two or three guava and cashew trees. With these fruits, we fed ourselves. When we were saturated we were again on our journey.

This time we went through the main road and passed a place called Ugwu Nzu in Mgbowo before entering into the bush again. There, some people who were tired withdrew themselves from the group. They were not told to go but to look after the animals that were captured now that it was too heavy for one person to carry. We jumped into the bush and soon, the attention of a bush rat was drawn to us. We went to the spot where it was and soon we found it running towards the side of a small stream. We chased it from all sides, and not wanting to be caught easily, it jumped into the water. This made the situation worse for soon all the hair became wet, and so it was captured easily.

We crossed the stream to see some monkeys playing up on the trees. With our catapult and big stones we wounded one which went away screaming. We pursued it but it went out of sight into the thick bush. We left it and went towards the Awgu side and, there, we wounded a dove badly, that it fell down after flying about ten yards, before lying still on the ground.

Now, we were nearing the place that we were going to rest. We finally reached there and everybody was glad and happy that nobody was wounded after the adventure. We soon settled down on the dwarf mud walls that held up the house. Some people were selected to cook the yams and some of the animals we caught. While they were busy cooking them, we were busy in our turn telling the story of what we had seen in the forest.

When the cooking was done, the share of the master who led us to the place was given to him, but he refused the offer because he had already eaten his two loaves of bread and a tin of geisha. The sharing was done and the share of some students given to them. Others were too inquisitive, impatient and too greedy to get their share. You know what the life of students was. They pounced on the foodstuff and were soon struggling over it. After the tussle, the master addressed us that it was bad manners to struggle over food, especially in the case in which people were passing frequently. When we had rested and had told 'bukas', we were ordered to get up, and were soon on our way back to school.

When we reached Ugwu Nzu which was at least five miles from our school we curved into the other side of the bush, to do the last phase of the hunting. There, some people dropped and others continued the journey. We had not hunted for a while when some people suggested that we should make fire. This was resisted by others but soon they too yielded to the request. Soon the fire was up, ravaging many bushes. It continued till it was almost unquenchable. We killed many animals at that place but what was the need for it because the fire was becoming too much. We got fresh leaves and started quenching it to the last. After an hour of serious work the fire went down so we made haste to go back to school at once.

On our way to the school we caught a chameleon on the leaves of a cassava. We picked it with the cassava stem and went with it to our school.

By the time we reached school it was about seven pm in the night. We went straight to our beds and did not say anything that night for if we started telling or vomitting or voicing our experience that day, it would take a whole day.

In the morning, during time for Assembly we showed the things we captured to the principal. He congratulated us well and said that we should keep it up. Some of the animals were eaten but others were taken to the school laboratory for experiments. Many chemicals were poured on some so that they would not rot. Up till today the animals are still there in the lab!

During the Inter-Science lesson, a rat's belly was cut open and an experiment carried out on it. All the master's teaching was good and true. The experiment was good but we suffered that day for the long journey, at least fourteen miles going and returning.

So ended the great hunting expedition in our school which I participated in.

Chapter Two

The Great Cross Country Race

In almost all secondary schools in the federation as a whole, morning Cross Country race has become the main exercise and sports in some ways. This sport has been existing for some time, and is interesting if it is done in the right way. This affects all the students of the institution, including the class five students, but whenever the West African Council Examination was approaching, the class five boys would be exempted. Excluding the class five students, all other students are included, except those that are not well and who would have reported to the senior prefect before the game starts. Except for these people mentioned no other person was excluded and if found doodling about the person's name will be written and submitted to the principal during the time of Assembly for punishment.

The day was Friday. School went on as before. When the school dismissed, everybody went back to their dormitories to do the remaining functions. After some casual work had been done the time for classes reached. After the afternoon's classes, everybody went to play. When the time for playing expired, other functions resumed. The class one and two boys that were fetching water did it; plates were passed, and immediately the sharing of food started. After resting for about twenty minutes, the Study Prefect announced that the time for classes had started. People carried their books and rushed down to the classrooms to occupy space in the classes. Five minutes to the end of the classes, the bell announced the warning bell for the junior ones. When the full bell had gone, every junior student assembled in front of the place they used as a praying ground.

Prayers over, the leading functionaries appeared and ordered that nobody should make noise. The functionaries were the Senior Prefect, the Game Captain, the Disciplinarian and the Labour Prefect. They announced that tomorrow's cross country race will be the best organized and the most magnificent in the history of the school. After about twenty minutes talk on how the race would be conducted, we remained quiet.

Above all, the prefects said that everybody should be in his white short and the school vest on top of it. If you have a canvas or any other cover shoes you will wear that, if not you go barefooted rather than wear slippers, To this, we answered, "Yes, Sirs," and were about to go when three boys stepped forward and said that they were not well. The other said that he was suffering from dislocation of the hand. He was inspected and found that he was telling the truth. The other boy was suffering from malaria for his body was like hot water. The last boy was asked what he was suffering from and he nearly laughed but held back. After he was inspected and it was found that nothing was wrong with him he was given six lashes of the cane and the SP told him to report to him immediately it was five o'clock in the morning.

After the exercise, everybody went back to his bed. Sooner or later everybody was dosing and snoring. When the time reached for the senior students to retire, they were also given their own lecture on the issue.

In the morning, around six am when the rising bell always went off, sounds of whistles were heard everywhere by those mentioned functionaries. Some class five students were still reading in the classroom. The Senior Prefect jumped into the classroom and seized all the books he could see. When everybody had appeared or assembled, some spies were sent to find out those that will dodge the race. We assembled according to our sizes. There were about four groups made up of about one hundred and twenty students in each group. The small ones were in the first group and the second group. The third group was made up of the middle sized people, while the last were the "old cargos" of the school. Everybody stood in fours.

As we ran down the avenue, some people suggested that we should go to Nnewe side while the greater number of the students said that we should go to Mgbowo side. The decision was taken and we were told to go to Mgbowo side because the road was much better than that of Nnewe side. We moved slowly, according to the orders of those controlling us. After about twenty yards of running we were told to raise any song we knew. Some suggested that one song, others suggested that one then the games captain told one boy to raise any song he knew quite well. He started it in the traditional Igbo language.

Ebe ka unu si
Awgu County,
Ebe-e ka unu si
Agwu County,
Agama arapu Awgu County
Gaba ebe ozo ga bili,
Aga ma arapu Awgu County
Ga ebe ozo ga bili
Awgu County ga di ndu.

In English, the song went as follows:

Where are you people from,
The chorus answered: Awgu County,
Where are you people from:
Awgu County,
I won't leave Awgu County
And go to any other place to live
I won't leave Awgu County
And go to any other place to live,
Awgu County shall live

This song continued until it was replaced with another one. The people became happy, and would have continued the journey but the games captain told us to turn back. We turned back towards the school side again, according to the order that we came, the juniors first and the seniors at the extreme back. We then resumed our running and were singing more vigorously than ever. The song which everybody knew all well went like this:

> Those that we are greater than,
> Those that we are greater than,
> You are insulting us,
> Those that we are greater than,
> (Here we named the neighbouring schools around us).
>
> Agbogwugwu Boys we are greater than those insulting us,
> Awgu Girls we are greater than those insulting us,
> [UgwuOkwute]
> Mgbowo Boys we are greater than are insulting us,
> Those that we are greater than

The song ran thus in Igbo language:

> Kwenu ndi anyi kaka,
> Ndi anyi kaka
> Kwenu ndi anyi kaka, ndi anyi kaka,
> Na aba ra anyi mba,
> Ndi anyi kaka,
> Agbogwugwu anyi kaka, na aba ra anyi mba,
> Ugwu Okwute anyi kaka, na abara anyi mba,
> Mgbowo Boys anyi kaka,
> Na abara anyi, mba,
> Kwenu di anyi kaka-a

When we got near the school compound the song changed to what we always call "operation feed the nation", in which song we praised the Head of State, the Military Governor of Anambra and Imo States, and also the senior officials of our school. This we sang until we reached inside the compound. When everything was settled, the names of those that dodged the race were submitted to the Senior Prefect who kept it.

During the time for assembly we all dashed there. The principal praised all the functionaries that made the race a successful one with a long speech. The Senior Prefect also handed the names of those that did not participate in the morning cross country race. Ten of them who were involved were called out. They were questioned but they could not give any answer. They were told to lie down, which they did. Twelve strokes of the cane were given to each one of them. After that they were told to dig a pit where rotten things were thrown into. Three great "hip, hip, hip!" were given to the students for the race was indeed a successful one.

So ended the greatest and the most exciting morning cross country race I had attended. The people who were bare-footed and were wounded by stones on the way were given First Aid from the school's First Aid box. When all things had been done, like praying and singing, we all disappeared to our respective classes for study.

Chapter Three
Disciplinary Matters I

After the death of a student of CIC Enugu, who was killed by his fellow school boy in class five, the Anambra Military Governor and the Anambra State School Management Board wrote a warning letter to all the principals in all the schools in the state to warn all the students of their school against fighting in the school which was growing too rampant. When the letter was issued to our principal we all knew that leaving the assembly will be around eleven am, for before the letter was issued he used to speak for more than two hours. Now that a circular was given it will rise to four hours. During time for Assembly he came quietly and said, "Good morning, students." We then answered him, "Good morning, Sir."

He spoke for some time concerning fighting in the school which he said was becoming too great, especially in the refectory because of food. When he had spoken for about five and a half hours he showed us the letter that came to his office from Enugu that morning. As he was reading it, we were listening and admiring the letter and its content. He closed it and gave the last warning before going out. The SP came and prayed. We then marched to our classes, singing the song one of our masters in the school taught us. The song was called, "When the students are marching on". When we dispersed to our classes there was no quarrel with anybody at all and nobody dared to make trouble. After some hours of lesson and learning, the school dismissed. The afternoon meal was taken and also the afternoon class was attended.

In the evening, almost in the night, when the time for sharing the evening meal was approaching, everybody went quietly to the refectory to pass his plate. Then the time for sharing started. All the people who it was their turn to share raced down the kitchen door to carry the food. When they finished sharing, everybody went to carry his food, but in our seat we were still sharing soup. After the "sharer" had finished sharing and was about to carry the bowl he used to share into the kitchen one ruthless boy held his food in his hand, saying that the sharer should not carry his food out.

It may be that the money of that boy had finished and he was not contented with the food they gave him or that he did want to fight and did not care about the principal's stern warning. The sharer told him to leave his food but he did not. On demanding to know what was wrong, he said that the sharer did not give him two pieces of meat. But really the sharer gave him two pieces of meat. The sharer was about to remove the hand of the boy from his plate when the food split on the floor. To make the matters worse the plate was a breakable plate. It landed on the ground and smashed into fragments.

The other boy's plate was also a breakable one, and so the sharer raised his leg and hit it on the offender's plate. The plate also broke. They two balanced, setting themselves into their boxing stance. Before anybody could know what was happening, fists were being exchanged. Exchanging fists for some time, they thought that it was no use so they pounced on each other and twisted themselves like wounded snakes. After about ten minutes of this struggle the offender was overpowered and was smashed to the floor like a log of wood that had fallen from the top of a big tree. The other boy pinned his hand with his knees and gave him some tremendous blows before any body could come to the scene.

After they were separated, the sharer gave him a heavy kick on the belly before he could stand up well. When he stood up soup had filled the back of his shirt and he was still struggling that they should leave him. Everything cooled down, and they were asked to state what the matter was. Discussions were held and it was found that the ruthless boy was the offender. Without wasting time, the boy was given twelve strokes of the cane and the sharer was given five strokes of the cane for going contrary to the principal's speech.

They were told to dismiss, and during time for classes everybody was discussing what will be the great judgment tomorrow by the principal, a well established man. After classes, the boy again hooked the sharer and said that now was the time for the real fighting. The sharer tried to remove his hand but the grip was tightening. He held the boy on the hands. As he did so, the boy gave him a deadly slap in which he saw stars. The sharer retaliated with two even more powerful ones such that the boy did not see for about two minutes. Before he could regain his full consciousness his face was full of bruises and had swollen up.

They were, this time, dragged to the Senior Prefect of the school. The SP ordered them to call their witnesses. The sharer called about six boys but the offender could not call any person because nobody would have been on his side if he ever called them. He was defeated again and told to go and cut a very big elephant grass that night, while the other boy was told to lie down for some time and told to go.

After the incident had ended everybody went to his bed. In the morning, during the time for Assembly, the Senior Prefect called them out again to answer for themselves regarding the case. They were also told to bring the broken plates with them. The principal, before judging the case, gave them six strokes each because they had gone contrary to his will within a day. Again, he said that it was not their plate but rather their parents who had used their money to buy those plates they had destroyed. He asked them to state what the case with them was. The sharer stated how there was no one to share in "our seat and I carried the food to the refectory to share. When I had finished sharing, everybody got two pieces of meat each. I knew that because I inspected them before I started sharing the soup. When I finished sharing and was about to carry my food this boy held it. I told him to leave the food, but he didn't. In the struggle to get my food, he threw the food to the floor and my plate broke. I then threw his own to the floor and it also broke and we started fighting."

The other boy was told to state what was wrong with him. He said that the boy did not give him two pieces of meat as was in the plate of others. The sharer called the table head who said that the sharer put in all the plates two pieces of meat and gave the remaining to the Labour Prefect which made his own three pieces of meat. The boy was given extra twelve lashes before he was told to go and pack his things from the dormitory and take his school transfer certificate and look for another school. Meanwhile, the other boy was given a piece of grass to cut for not reporting to the Senior Refectorian before he took matters into his own hand.

The principal also used this incident to warn students against fighting in the school compound. He warned about exchanging harsh words, not to talk of anybody fighting with his neigbhour. Should that happen, he admonished, such a person will have himself to blame. He said that the boy was a scapegoat, and that he used him to set an example for others who will not heed his warning. He said that he will write a letter to the State School Management Board concerning the expelled boy.

Three days after the boy's departure, he called his parents to come and plead for him in the principal's office. His father came with a written apology, together with the boy's written apology to the principal. When the principal went through that letter he nodded and told the father to go. Before he left, he warned them that if the boy was found doing or involving himself in any form of trouble in the school that the matter will be worse. He, finally, told the boy to go and get back all his things again. He received the transfer certificate from him. So ended the great fight in the refectory.

Chapter Four
The Great Football Match

One day, during the time for Assembly, the Games Master came back from Enugu on his motorcycle, together with a piece of paper in his hand. He came near the Assembly ground and stopped his motorcycle. He had a letter in his hand, and greeted us in the normal way before he started to read the letter. The letter indicated that football practice should start as from that day during the time for long break because he said that we were going to play Agbogwugwu Boys in both junior and senior categories.

So, after the time for Assembly, the junior boys entered the field – first the old players were chosen, and some new ones were taken to complete us. Some played badly but others did better, although for the past two months we had never practised. Changes were made until after about a week's time, the first and second eleven boys were known. When it was three days to the great day we played as we had never played before. Unfortunately for me I got wounded that day. (That wound made it impossible for me to take part in the match).

The day before the match the jerseys were washed, together with the 'tug.' The 'international jerseys' were put in a different place for junior boys while the other one was for the senior boys. On the day of the event there was no school. Two days before the match, a van contracted by our school developed trouble around 1:30 pm. By the time we were ready to start, the van appeared on the scene. About thirty players jumped in, together with the Games Captain and the Games Master who took their seats in the front seat. About twenty minutes of the arrival of the van we were on the move, making sure that we left nothing behind. The place was about ten miles so that the driver increased the speed of the van so as to reach there in time. After about twenty-five minutes, we arrived at the place. When we entered the school, eyes were set on us. We jumped down as the van stopped.

On disembarking, we were told to stay at one place by our officials. Our boys were told to run round the field so as to get themselves warm before the match. After the exercise, the Agbogwugwu Boys appeared on the field. After they had taken their positions, the referee told them the rules and blew the whistle. The game started. Our opponents were on the offensive because our boys had never played on the field before, which was full of small pebbles. There was a time I said that they will score a goal against our own side. It was on the twenty-fifth minute of the play. The centre forward for the Agbogwugwu Boys dribbled one of our defenders and played a tremendous shot at our goal post. The goal keeper was fast enough to punch the ball away and it went over the bar, with a little space between the bar and the goal post. After a series of exciting play, the first half ended in a draw.

Our boys were escorted out of the field so that they will rest. Glucose was given to them. They were also told to try hard and score one goal. Some changes were also made. When the referee blew his whistle for the second half our boys entered with full determination that they will score a goal that time. During the second half, the ball was always at the midfield for every side was determined to score a goal. Then, the ball came to the possession of one of our boys. He beat a man, beat another, and in an instant a banana shot came through but it went over the bar. That time, there was a round of applause from the spectators.

A free kick was taken by one of their boys. It bounced at the centre of the field and some people scrambled for the possession of the ball. The last straw that broke the camel's back came in the thirty-eight minute of the second half when one of our boys called Victor took possession of the ball. He kicked the ball up and a man came. He beat him with his head. As the ball was coming down a level shot came and lo! It was a goal.

There were shouts and clapping. Joy came again when they passed the ball after we scored. Every side was determined to clear every mess. Their boys were on the offensive again, while our men kept on using delay tactics. When the match ended it was 1-0 against Agbogwugwu boys.

Then came the turn of the senior boys. Their own was less interesting than the junior ones. They played as they had never played before. In the twenty-eighth minute of play, our boys scored a goal against them. They thought that they had won but as the first half was about to end there was a struggle at our goal post resulting in a 'corner kick'. The ball was scrambled for, and finally it entered our goal. The first half ended 1 - 1. The second half was less exciting than the first half. Both sides played delay tactics until the game ended.

We were waiting for the van that conveyed us to the place when their Games Master called all the players back. We all moved to the place where we were called to. It was a large classroom with seats and lockers. We took our seats and waited for what was going to happen. Immediately, two big boys carried in a basin of jollof rice. Then, followed another. The last came with a small basin full of fried meat. Plates were also provided, together with some spoons. The plates were filled with rice and some pieces of meat before it was distributed to us. When we finished eating, palm wine (tombolikwo) or 'booze' was brought out from where it was kept, together with two cartons of Becks beer. Cups were also provided, and we drank to our satisfaction.

After the merriment, our Games Master told us and all the Agbogwugwu boys to go outside so that he can address us. He gave the address and praised the Games Master of the school for what he had done. The man in his reply said that it was nothing, that we were all brother schools. They bade us farewell and a safe journey. We went away but the question was which van will we use to go now that the one we hired had not come back, and it was about 8 pm in the night. We came to the side of the main road to find that the place was filled with people; students from our school who were waiting for the van which will convey them. Any car that drove past did not even look our way for fear of thieves and the bad attitude of students. After some time, a tipper came. It was waved down. The driver stopped slowly so that he will know what sort of people were stopping him.

When he saw that it was students and they were pleading, he told us to enter but said that we should pay him 20kobo each. We agreed and jumped in. The lorry started slowly, but within a short time it gathered speed. As we were running on a straight road, we saw the van we hired coming from Awgu side. We stopped it. We all got down without paying the man. He was angry. We entered the other bus, but he stood in front of it and said the bus should not move unless we pay him what was agreed.

So, we all climbed out from the bus and paid the man his due. We told the driver we hired that there were still students in the school compound of the place we played football and told him to go and collect them. Meanwhile, we climbed inside the lorry again and he drove us towards our school compound. On getting to school, we raised a song in Igbo which went thus :

Those that don't know
How to play football
Said that we should play football,
Then, what happened?
When we played it,
Agbogwugwu have learnt a lesson.

This, we sang until we entered the school compound and told the others that did not go what had happened. As we were saying this the other van arrived with the remaining group of people at Agbogwugwu. They, too, climbed down and walked with us inside the compound. We told the story to those that did not go to the match, after which we passed our plates and refreshed our memory again with food. We had no intention to go to class to read, but went quietly to our beds because we were tired.

So ended the great football match between our school and Saint Vincent Secondary School, Agbogwugwu.

Chapter Five
Great School Societies

In all secondary schools there were, at least, about five societies. These societies had different functions to perform in the institution in which they exist. In almost all secondary schools in the federation the reigning society, and the society loved by a great many people was the debating society. Some people loved it because of the dance with girls from other schools, while other because of the debate that was made before the main dance. Yet, others still because of the merriment that was made before any debating agenda that will take place. Lastly, a great portion because the food prepared for the girls will be left after the girls had finished eating, and they will go and eat the remaining.

The second respected society in most schools was the geographical society. Some people like it because of the wonderful places they visited during excursions. Other people like it because of the towns visited during the exercise. Again, some loved it because they had not travelled distant places a lot, so they wanted to travel on a long journey.

The third one was the cultural society. This cultural society was a new society introduced in secondary schools but in the little time it was introduced, it had become almost the master of all societies in all schools. These people always danced the traditional and cultural dance called 'Atilogwu' dance. They always featured during festive days like the welcoming and send off of principals, the children's day and the Independence Day anniversary celebration.

Then, followed the Young Christian Society. This was very much like the debating society only that they did not debate. The students nicknamed them the "Young criminal society" There was also dance in it, but in the place of debate as in the debating society, they had "drama" to present.

Under this column, I will state the occasions the above mentioned societies featured in which I was a witness. Let me first of all start with the debating which, as I had mentioned above, was the best loved society in the school.

1. Debating Society: Junior:
One day as we were listening in the Assembly ground, because the SP was calling out letters, one boy who we had known well as the President of the Junior Debating Society whispered something to the SP's ear. We did not know what it was. After the SP had finished calling out the letters, he said that all the members of the Junior Debating Society will have a meeting in class 3A classroom after the afternoon's meal; that was around or between 2pm – 3pm. He said that 'day students' should also attend for some were members, and also new members were welcome. After the announcement, we all retired to the classrooms to read.

Immediately we finished taking our food, all the members of the Junior Debating Society went to class 3A block. We were all seated and the president wrote something on the black board which ran thus:

Agenda
1. Admission of new members
2. The school we shall invite
3. The amount that should be paid by new members
4. The amount that should be paid for the show.
5. Election of some officials
6. Other matters that should arise

The matters were attended to and new members were asked

to pay 50kobo each, after which there will be another due which was ₦1.50kobo for the show that will take place in a fortnight. Some officials were duely elected. Now came the question of the school that will be invited. Some suggested this school, others suggested that school. After all was said and done, it was agreed that we will invite Oghe Girls.

Two days after the meeting, the president and the financial secretary went and got an order from the principal so that the school driver will use the school van to convey them to Oghe Girls. After much persuasion the principal agreed. So, the van took them to the school. When they came back they said that everything was set. We summoned another meeting which was again attended. There was written on the board the opposing side and the proposing side – the words ran like this: Polygamy Should Not Be Encouraged.

S/No.	Proposing Side	Opposing Side

Volunteers were called and we set to learn the debate topic. Our practice was better compared with others we had done before.

After a week and four days of learning, the great day remained only one day to approach. The day before that day, we swept the school hall, carried chairs in it, together with some tables for the judges and the officials. The compound was also kept tidy.

At last came the 'D-day'. Around 11:20am the 'soundman' came and showed that he was around by playing some records. When he came, everybody made haste to prepare for the occasion.

Around 1:30pm, the girls came in their school bus and one other bus. They were escorted round the school premises by some people.

They were then led to their eating place. After they had eaten, the remains were scrambled for by hungry and greedy students. They were led back to the hall. They judges were already seated. The master of ceremony then made a speech and called the opposing side, that is; the girls to come out and support their idea. The lead debater came out and made a brief speech on the issue. She was applauded. This continued until the debate finished. Everybody was now listening to the decision of the judges. They declared that it was a draw game– 6 - 6 points each. Some soft drinks were served the girls and the main thing started. We danced as we have never danced before. We danced 'whole self' also because the girls were too romantic. We danced until about 5pm when the girls said that they were going. They went back to their van and bade us goodbye. During the dance I managed to get one 'chick' as my girlfriend. So did others. After the show, the seats were carried back to the classrooms and the house was thoroughly swept. So everything became normal again. So ended the debating show I had witnessed.

ii. Geographical Society:
One morning, as we were reading in the classroom, the geographical society master came to each class to announce that there was going to be a meeting in class 5B classroom. So, during the long break, at the above mentioned time, we all went there. He said that in every first term, that we will always have an excursion. He said that for this year's own he will suggest that we go to the 'Umuahia Brewery Company'. This was agreed to without any objection. He also said that we were going to pay ₦2.50kobo each, going and returning. We all agreed that we will pay ₦2.50kobo each and waited for the travelling day to come. We dismissed with the conclusion that it was the 'Uhuru Transport Limited' that was going to convey us to the place. We went back to our classes; every one of us.

On that day, that was a Friday, we prepared before the bus came, and took with us any amount that each one of us thought that will be suitable for him on this long journey. The food was shared early because of our going because we intended to leave the school compound around 7am in the morning. At last, came the big and beautiful yellow bus that will be ours that day. The master leading us introduced himself to the driver and his mates who, in turn, introduced themselves to him. The master stood at the door of the bus and called the names of those going, according to the order of payment.

My love for the geographical society made me pay early, so that I was the 4th person to pay. When I was called I jumped in. This continued until the names finished. The master told the driver to begin with the journey. The bus moved slowly and we waved to the students standing by the way side. After we travelled for about 1 hour 30 minutes I fell asleep. On waking up, I found that we were in Umuahia township. Soon we stopped in front of a signboard captioned with some words like: 'Welcome to the Umuahia Brewery Company.'

We all jumped down and gazed at the sight we saw. The master led us inside the compound of the industry. The Director-General came and explained certain things to us, especially how the beer was made. He soon called a man who led us inside the industry. It was impossible to describe what we saw or what we heard in the mysterious place, but two places which attracted my admiration will be mentioned. One was the place I thought there was no air inside it except for the air conditioner. The place was cold to the extent that I thought that I was no longer alive. Indeed, I tried to run out but I thought that was a Stone Age man's idea.

Another place was the place in which bottles were running in hundreds and in thousands, struggling for their way. It was an astonishing and amazing sight to see. When the show ended we all went back to our bus. We were given chance to buy anything that time. Some climbed down, while others remained. I climbed out and bought an ice cream. One boy bought a loaf of bread and a tin of milk. When he finished eating them he started vomitting. By his looks one could see that he was a native of an interior part of the state.

Soon, we were on the way to our school. As we were going, one boy started to sing one meaningless song, which ran like

this:
   Sa na chan sa chan
   Sa na chan sa chan
   Sa na chan sa chan
   Sa na chan sa chan
   Sa na chan sa chan

Immediately everybody started to sing it until we entered the school compound. That night we told our mates what we had seen

iii. Dramatic and YCS Societies:
These two societies were like the debating society but differed in some ways. For example, in YCS, they did not make any debate but just danced and made merriment. In Dramatic society, instead of debating, they performed any play they knew. No need saying anything on them, because my advice is for one to go and study the debating society, and he will learn about these two societies the more.

iv. Cultural Society:
This society was newly formed but within a short time it had grown in importance. They showed their display on the day our old principal was sent off and the new one welcomed. When the speeches by the two principals and the Senior English Master had finished, they took off. They danced as they had never danced before. They showed all the styles they knew, but the most interesting one in the acrobatic display was the building of 'upstairs' with people. Everybody clapped their hands and money was thrown to them by the non officials like mad. After that, little dance was made. When everything finished everybody went away. The refectory bell was heard, so people marched to have their share.

So ended the great societies' activities in the school.

Chapter Six

Sports in My School

i. In our school the most respected day was the day of the Inter-house sports. It was this day that will be decided the winner of the cup donated by one man from the town in which the school was [Nnewe]. It was this day also that the school will celebrate its anniversary, so as to remember the day the school was opened. The 18th Anniversary Inter-House Sports in which we struggled for the Chief Nwonye's cup was the most magnificent in all the Inter-house sports, and other sports I had ever attended or witnessed.

When it was made known to us that it was about three and a half weeks before the sports will take place we all tried all our possible best so as to make it a successful one. We, first of all, cleared the field in which it was going to take place. The tracks were marked, together with the shot put pit, the javelin pit, the discus pit, the long jump pit, the pole vault arena, the high jump pit and the triple jump pit. The Games Master drafted on the school notice board the order of practice for each house. This practice continued until it was two days to the day.

The following day, the 'heat' was held in all the events. In the 100 metres heat I came second. Also in the 200 metres, I also came second. In the evening of that day, all the tracks were white washed, both for the track and field events. That day, also, all the houses were told to get some palm fronds and palm leaves so as to make huts for each house. Already, a large booth was made for the spectators and the officials as well.

In the morning of that day, the booth was filed with plenty of invitees. Around 11am in the morning a march past was conducted by the Games Master for all the houses in the school, beginning with the winning house the previous year, Ikpenwa house. After that, the main event started. It was the senior boys 100 metres. They all got set and, at the sound of the whistle, they were off. Before they reached the stopping point our house representative became the winner. In the junior boys 100 metres, I also came first. So did I in the 200 metres junior boys. Our man equally came first in the 200 metres senior boys. We were leading in the track event all together, but when it came to field events we became second.

When all the events had finished, on the notice board was written, Onwe House came first with 98 points; Ibiam House came second with 89 points. Ibiam house was my house. Since this house was formed it never reached 4th position, but now the situation had changed. I, alone, got more than 21 points.

Then came the distribution of prizes by the Chair Lady. When everything finished the winning house captain was presented with the Nwonye Cup. He, with his members, ran off joyfully with their masquerade and the silver cup.

Back at our house we were drinking the 'tombolikwo' we had purchased. After that, everybody disappeared to his bed.

ii. The inter-house matches were good games but not better than the Inter-house sports. These matches between one house and the other continued until, at last, the winner emerged.

When the match started, every house was determined to win. The first house that played was Ikpenwa vs. Ibiam house. They were defeated by 3 – 0. We again defeated two other houses. At last, it remained Onwe house and our house. That evening the sides of the field were filled with students, natives and our school masters as well. When the match started, we were being pressed badly because the wind was blowing hard and was against us. They played and played but no side scored. At one time, the ball came to possession of one of our player who beat their defender. He gave one shot. It flew over the bar. Another one again hit the bar and the third time it, again, went over the bar.

The Onwe boys became more and more enthusiastic to score a goal. They collected the ball, passed it to their player who carried the ball down the far right wing of the field and crossed it. There was a scramble for the ball at our goal post resulting in one of our defender who, in the mission of playing the ball away, played it inside our goal post. The onlookers shouted with joy as the ball entered the net. Our boys carried the ball out to pass it. As they passed it, our centre forward played the ball to our outside right who crossed the ball. The ball hit their defender on the head and went over the bar. The referee blew the whistle for a corner kick. As it was taken one of our boys jumped high in the air and put the ball inside the net with his head which made the score 1 – 1. When they passed the ball every side was determined to score now, but no goal was scored again in the first half. The referee blew the whistle for the end of the first half.

After the short interval between the end of first half and the beginning of the second half, the referee blew his whistle for the second half. They all entered the field with few changes. From the start of the second half to the end the ball was a one-sided game against the Onwe boys. Their goalkeeper was always in the advance to catch the ball while our men were always in possession of the ball. In the 15th minute of the second half we scored our second goal. They made changes again but it was all in vain. We pressed them hard and nearly scored four times but the ball was always hitting the bar. It was like if medicine was put in their goal post. On the fifth instant our inside left scored our third goal in the 30th minute of the play. From that 30th minute to the 45th minute no side again scored. They were struggling to score while our men were using delay tactics.

When the referee blew his final whistle the members of our house jumped into the field to carry our men shoulder high in the air. We carried them, shoulder high. As we were going we were singing in Igbo:

Ikpenwa, shouted, shouted, and woke up the lion,
Alinta shouted, shouted, and woke the lion,

Ziks shouted, shouted, and woke up the lion
Nwonye shouted, shouted, and woke the lion,
Ezeanya shouted, shouted, and woke up the lion,
Onwe shouted, shouted, and woke up the lion,
When the lion awoke,
Bad thing will happen.

We also sang the song which we sang during the cross country race:-

Agree, those that we are stronger than,
Agree, those that are stronger than all the other houses, We are greater than,
Those that we are greater than,
[The song was sang in Igbo, you know.]

When we finished singing and rejoicing, the gigantic cup was presented to the captain of our house. We carried it round the houses and the masters' quarters.

iii. The Inter L.G.A. all sports competition was much like the Inter-house sports competition, only that the case of Inter L.G. competition comprised all the schools in the Local Government Area, while in the Inter house sports it was only our school that took part. Also, in the Inter L.G.A. competition, certificate was presented while in the Inter-house sports competition prizes were presented to the winners of each event.

So, ended sports activities in our school.

Chapter Seven
Social Vices in the School

In my first year in secondary school I have been hearing of 'apian way' and 'PMB,' which they called 'public male band' against the original name, Private Mail Bag. This 'apian' something was popular but the meaning, I could not think of.

During the holidays, I asked one of my friends in another institution whether he knew what was being called 'apian way'. He said that he has heard of it but did not know the meaning of the ugly word.

One day, in our school, something made me to, at last, know what 'apian way', and especially 'PMB'. were. It was when about twenty boys were called out in the assembly ground by the Senior Prefect. The charges against them were that they were caught in Mgbowo town in the night, attending a marriage ceremony. When this was said, I, at once knew the meaning of 'Public male band' and 'apian way'.

This was what happened. Whenever there was a marriage ceremony, especially on Saturdays, I did not know how these people managed to know that there was a marriage ceremony. They will sneak out, unnoticed. This continued to happen until one day the Senior Prefect was in front of his cubicle reading, when he saw a group of people going down the avenue of the school. He sent a spy who pretended to be going with them. He took with him a book and a pen. As they were going he was telling them that today was his first time of going to that place in his life. He said that he wanted to join them in their secret society, called 'PMB society'.

The person who appeared to be the leader of the gang

introduced to him how the operation should be carried out. He told him that if they reach they should not be calling anybody by his real name but by 4 – 2 names. He told him that they who had been going to the place had girlfriends they used any how they liked. He told him to struggle to get one friend who he will be dealing with when they go the next time.

When he asked them how they knew that there was 'PMB', he said that it may be by the sound of the music, where it was coming from or in the evening of every Friday each of the member will volunteer himself to go to Mgbowo and ask to know whether there was any 'PMB' the following Saturday. He nodded and they went on.

When they reached the place he, the spy, said that will he won't be able to dance. They told him to sit on top of a heap of blocks used there for building. From there he was able to write all their names without being noticed. When he finished writing the names he put the book into his pocket again and waited for the time they will go. When they reached where he was they woke him up and they started their journey back to the school compound. As they were going one boy said 'egburu mie to-o-to-o'[I really dealt with her]. They kept on saying how they danced with the girls until they reached the school compound.

They all went back to their respective dormitories and from there to their beds. In the morning, during time for assembly, they were all surprised to find their names being called out in the assembly ground. They were given twelve strokes each by about nine masters after which they were given a place to dig as a punishment.

In another instance, students were fond of going to the town to drink wine. This reminded me of the incident which happened when I was in class three; of one boy who went to his friend's place to drink wine. His friend was a day student. If he had drank the one he could carry it would have been better, but the worse of it was that he drank over one full big bottle of 'kai-kai'.

When he returned to the school compound he was no longer with his senses. He destroyed some seats, and even used them to scatter students watching the football match going on. He pursued everybody he saw. He was doing this because he was badly seized by this powerful wine so that he went and lay in the dormitory. Around 8pm in the night, when the SP was inspecting to know those that did not go to the class to study, the boy was unconscious. The SP gave him about 10 strokes of the cane. He did not even attempt touching the place he was being caned. By that time he had vomitted in almost the whole of the dormitory.

His dress was pulled off and he was given a thorough sprinkling of water to the body but still he could not shake his head. Everybody was just giving up hope when he opened his eyes and closed it again. After some time he was carried and locked up in a dormitory that was reserved for class one students. When he was there the place was locked until the following morning. In the morning he came out well, and when he was told what happened yesterday he did not believe it but said that it was a false story.

Now, below is the full text on the issue: to start with, let me first of all talk about those people that form the habit of going to 'PMB' and using the 'apian way'. What do they derive from this silly act? They derive nothing. They only go there and mess up, and also brought bad name to the school. The trouble was that it was those people that went to the so-called 'PMB' and used the 'apian way' that committed 'expo' and even failed in their examinations. In our class, at least, four boys failed because of this 'PMB'. Do they mean that on the examination day that 'PMB' will come and write for them in the examination hall?

This warning goes directly to the class one boys who had entered the school new so that they would not attempt to go to the 'PMB'. I could remember one day when one boy was caught going to the 'PMB' in the night. He was told to do 'aeroplane turner' that night and also sing:

> I will never go to the 'PMB'. again
> I will never go to the 'PMB'. again,
> It is not good to go there.
> I promise that I will never go there again
> Until I leave this school.

This he continued dancing and singing and running about

until he nearly fainted. Such was the fate of those going to 'PMB', so I advice anybody that will enter a secondary school, and also those that will read this book to keep away from this evil act called 'Public male band' and using the so-called 'apian way'. Beware of it, or it will ruin your mind. But if you insist, you will have yourself to blame for there is an Igbo saying which states:

> "Ekwekwe na ekwe na utara ekwere ekwe,"( ) and there is another one, "hot water 'de' kill tortoise or Mbe".

In our school the obedience of students was the same as that of other institutions in the state or federation. The chief law giver in the school was the principal. The law enforcement agencies were the functionaries, while the law breakers were the same students.

1. In the case of eating in the refectory, the principal said that nobody should eat in the dormitory, but in the refectory, be the person in class 100. This address was given in the assembly ground. When the school dismissed, the school senior functionaries called another meeting to warn the students again about what the principal said. During time for eating you can still see some students carrying their food into the dormitory, especially class five students. This resulted one day in a fight between the acting senior refectorian and one class five student. After that, the student was suspended.

2. Another great incident was that the morning assembly was a compulsory routine for every student in the institution. The principal had warned several times on this issue, and so did the school functionaries. Yet, during the time for assembly, if you go to Omuo stream, especially, or the bush at the back of the latrine, you will find many students hanging around. Some even lock themselves up in the toilet. What was the need of hiding during the time for assembly? Have these people who are dodging assembly any sense at all? This led to the principal forming some students into 'disciplinary squads'. The main work of this group

was to go about in the bush or in the stream to catch any lawbreaker. Those hiding were caught in great number and given severe or tedious punishment. Now that they were caught, where do they hide again?

3. The third offence was jumping through the window, especially during the time for classes. Some students had formed the habit of jumping through the window during time for classes, especially the class five students. Some students even were fond of staying in the dormitory during time for classes. A greater number of them wander or loiter about in every place when classes were going on. Some even formed the habit of reading in the bush during the time for classes. Some stay on the bank of the stream on the pretext of going to drink water. The most alarming thing was that these people, if they did this thing and were not caught, it would have been better, but they were doing it and yet, they were caught and given a thorough beating or a severe punishment.

4. Some students had formed the habit of not going to the school toilet to pass away the waste product. They were fond of going to shit in the farm of the masters. This they continued to do everyday, especially those responsible for fetching water to the kitchen – those were the class one and two students. When they will be going to the stream around 5:50am in the morning, they will just divert to the farm to do this mischief.

Another set of people that did these things were class five students who will read far in the night. They won't even go to the farm, not to talk of the school toilet. They will just go outside the class and pass away the waste product. On the morrow, the members of the class in which the waste product was deposited will be punished. Even when they read far into the night in the dormitory they will come outside and shit at the back of the dormitory. There was one day I woke up around 2 am to urinate at the back of the dormitory, I saw a class five student shitting there.

5. With regard to the case of shitting in the farm, there was a day

a class one student went to the stream early in the morning. He dropped his bucket at the side of the road and went inside a master's farm to shit. When the master came out of his house, he shone his torch on the boy who ran away, leaving behind the bucket, towel and the soap dish he was carrying. The master picked them and dropped them in his house. Two days later the boy came back to the man's house to plead that the things were his.

He was told to remove the shit. After that, he was given a piece of land to cut with a sharpened machete before he could get back his bucket and other things. He did as he was told before he got the bucket and other things

6. Another habit some students had formed which was bad was to dodge the manual labour on Wednesdays and on Fridays, together with the work boarders did on Tuesdays and Thursdays. Some students did always go to the marketplace to hide themselves during the time for work. Some went to Omuo stream to hide. Others climbed tree tops, while others went to the bush. There was one boy who was bitten by a scorpion on the leg when he was hiding in the bush. He screamed home to the school compound. He was asked to tell what happened to him but he could not and started to tell lies. He was not attended to until he confessed that he was hiding in the bush when the scorpion bit him on the left leg.

There was one boy who was hiding on a treetop. When he saw the senior prefect coming towards the direction he was, he made haste to come down before the prefect could come near. As he was struggling to come down fast, he miscalculated his steps and fell down. He could not walk, although his legs were not broken. The SP came to the site to see him. He went back and called some big students who carried him back to the school compound.

Why have some students formed the habit of altering the school's laws? Do they think that those who made these laws are foolish people? Unless students stop this silly act it will continue from generation to generation. As the principal said, if class five

77

students were doing bad things, when the class one students will reach to that stage, they too will say that when they were in class one that those class five students were misbehaving so that they too can misbehave

So, the suggestions, the warning and the address, were for class one students not to involve themselves on any of the above mentioned acts. They should abide by the school laws until they finish their course of study in the school.

Chapter Eight
Disciplinary Matters II

Thanks to the Anambra State Government and the State School Management Board for providing the caution fees deposit. This issue must also be attended to because, before the caution fees deposit or verdict, some students were living the kind of life called 'vandalism'. This means that they had destroyed many valuable things sent to them by the government.

Before anything was heard about caution fees, some students had taken it as their duty to destroy every amenity sent to them by the Anambra State Government. After all, they will say, "it is not my property but government's property". Again, before the caution fees verdict, students had been siding with the vandals. For example, if any student committed an offence without being seen by any of the officials, the students there will cover up for the person, but when the caution deposit appeared it was no longer like that. Two examples can be shown when the caution fees deposit had not appeared, and also two examples will be shown when the caution fees deposit was paid.

1. When the caution fees had not been paid, one evening, about nine boys were playing in a park which was like a field but was not. Although the original field was not occupied, beside the place in which they were playing was the school laboratory which was made of glass window and door. As these people were playing one boy, whether mistakenly or not, played a banging shot which went to the direction of the window and broke two panes. When the people playing looked around they did not see an official or any other person coming. They 'dodged' the ball and went away.

2. One afternoon, after the afternoon's meal, two boys were seen fighting in front of the classroom. Although nobody knew the cause of the fight, one of them, the bigger boy, hit the other left and right mercilessly. The other, in turn, bent down and picked a big stone, which he flung at the tormentor, who was lucky enough to dodge before the stone could reach him. The stone flew, and in the next instant hit the glass window of the class. Immediately the incident happened, the fighting stopped. The two became friends again because of the broken window.

But one morning, as the principal approached the assembly ground everybody knew that something was wrong. He greeted, "Good morning, students". We in turn greeted him, "Good morning, Sir". He read the letter from the State Government concerning the caution fees of 20 naira for each student. When he said that every student will pay 20 naira each, there were angry shouts and whistling from the students but they were calmed down by the approach of five masters with 'agha' cane in their hands. Within two days of the principal's speech and announcement everybody had paid his own. Now, if people were found playing expensive jokes the student there will shout, "caution fee," "caution fee."

3. One day, on a Wednesday, as we were in the class trying to go out for the manual labour, the labour prefect came to the class to ask us what we had been doing. We all jumped out through the window. As one boy was jumping out, the edge of his machete mistakenly hit the glass window which broke into fragments. The boy was dragged to the principal and money was subtracted from his caution fee.

4. As we were reading in the class, one of the florescent tubes was 'shining and stopping'. One boy mounted on top of the locker to see if he can repair it. As he was pushing it this way and that, the florescent tube dropped to the floor and broke. There was shout of "caution fee," "caution fee". The boy was dragged to the principal in the morning by the Senior Prefect, for one English proverb says, "it is better to be alone than to follow bad company."

The boy was asked to go and get the price of the tube in the market place. He went and said that it was five naira. The principal told him to buy it with his money which he did without hesitation. Another one was bought, which was used to replace the broken one.

Students should beware about how they use school property. This warning directly goes to class one students because they don't know much about the school affairs. "Don't follow bad company".

Chapter Nine
The Send-off of the Class Five Students

The month was May, the West African Examination for class five students had started. Everybody looked forward to the send-off party of the finalists which was always celebrated when the examination had gone half-way.

In the assembly, the assistant Senior Prefect announced that from the next Monday all students in class one to three will pay one naira for the send-off party while class four students who were sending the class five students off will pay ₦1.20kobo each. That day was Friday, so anybody who had his own will have to sign his exit card for permission to leave and collect his money. Those who had their own kept it in a safe place for fear of robbery. Those whose homes were near the school waited on Sunday which was the 'free day' so that they will go to their homes after mass to collect their own.

Exactly after school that day some students were streaming to the staff room to sign their exit cards from different house masters. On Sunday, a greater number of students left for their houses after church or mass. Some who had their money remained in the school compound discussing the past year's event, and of how a boy was 'gisting' or 'hunting' a girl and was largely refused.

On Monday, the money was duly collected by all the functionaries through the class prefects, but they got reports that there were still some stubborn and obstinate ones who refused to pay their dues. The shirts of such boys were seized, and they also received several strokes of the cane. Those affected all went into the dormitories during the time for long break to collect theirs.

About four days time, after the collection of the money had been completed, the plans for the party started immediately. The school senior functionaries also had a meeting in class 4A classroom to decide the fate of the show that was going to take place in about a week and four day's time. They suggested how the show should be organized so that it will be a success. Then they named the schools to be invited during the send-off party.

The schools were Saint Vincent Secondary School, Agbogwugwu, Oghe girls, Achi girls, Awka girls and Ngwo girls. In all of these schools, sixty persons were invited from each school, except Agbogwugwu in which forty guys were invited. They named the articles that should be bought. Furthermore, personalities to be invited were also mentioned.

On their second meeting they discussed the appearance of the whole compound and students on that day. The named the boys that should serve the guests that day. I was among them. It was also agreed that class one and two students should wash the toilets and the bathrooms while class three students should keep the whole compound clean.

When it remained three days to the great day, all the things needed were at hand. Meanwhile, the people who were sent to invite the girls came back with success stories. The day before the send off party, the school toilets were washed. The compound was kept clean by the people affected. The school hall was swept by some class one students while the main body of the class one and two students streamed into the hall with chairs and some tables.

Around 7am the following morning, the cooking of the food stuffs started. By 12pm or noon, the food was ready in the plates waiting for the eaters. We, the servers, were in the school store preparing bread and sardine stew there.

You know there is an Igbo saying, "The person blowing the whistle will, at one time, blow his nose, together with his mouth." So, when we did about five each, we will eat one. When we finished, we washed our hands, waiting for the guests.

Around 12:30pm the Awka girls arrived in a luxurious bus. They were followed by Ngwo girls who came in the same kind of bus. Third came the Agbogwugwu boys. Achi girls followed, together with Oghe girls. When all these people arrived, they were escorted round the school compound by some people, who showed them the buildings in the school compound and their uses. When the whole exercises ended, the 'nutrition' began in about 5 or 4 classrooms. They all took their seats.

We first served them with the main food of jollof rice with some pieces of meat in it. When they had finished, the food was carried out, and in came the wine. For the girls it was, fanta, coca cola and sprite. The boys were served can beer or lager beer. When the exercise ended, they were escorted out again, and into the school hall they went. We ate to our satisfaction the food the invitees left behind. We were followed by greedy and hungry students who scrambled over the leftover food.

Back at the hall, the guests and the officials had seated comfortably. The M.C. of the show introduced the chairman and some other responsible persons. Then, the A.S.P. stepped out to read the welcome address as well as the send-off address.

He spoke as he had never spoken before, his words sounding well and good. He looked at this direction and then at that direction.

He began by saying –

> Good afternoon, Mr. Chairman, officials, guests and the whole students as well. Today, we are going to make the ceremony of sending the recent finalists off in this school ...

When he had finished reading the pamphlet, there was loud clap of hands. The principal also made a speech as well before the main thing started. The serving of bread, groundnuts and biscuits followed immediately after the addresses. When they had tasted the merriment objects we carried them back to the school store so that it can be consumed. The sound man showed that he was in by raising to its highest volume, 'Papa's Land' by Sonny Okosuns– Ozzidism. When the sound of music came on, students stepped out to dance, the boys saying, "Excuse me dance," to the girls. As was the custom, the class one and two students were told to go out, but still some of them managed to stay unnoticed.

When about seven songs had been played, the minds of everybody were again refreshed with drinks.

When the time for 'whole self' reached, the M.C. said in the loud speaker, "I am going to set the hall warm with Bongos Ikwue and the Groovies, 'Baby Let Me Go'. When the music was booming, murmurings and low voices were heard from almost all angles, of boys 'tuning chicks' or girls. "Your choice" followed when the time for 'whole self' had expired. (All the boys will sit down; the girls will be standing up. When they were dancing, anybody that it was your choice, you will call that person out).

They danced and danced until it reached evening. Then, all the girls prepared to go. As they all went into their buses we waved them good bye. When their buses started to move they waved back to us in a joyous manner. When the show ended class one and two students carried back the chairs and the tables into the classrooms again. We were divided into two groups; one group swept the school hall while our own group swept the classroom in which the guests had eaten.

That evening, now that the cooks did not cook any food, the bell was rung to assemble the students. When we came we were told get our plates which we did without hesitation. The remaining food was shared among us. After eating, we sat in front of our dormitories discussing the recent send-off party the class five students had as we saw it.

Chapter Ten
Disciplinary Matters III

The following issue was half dealt with in chapter eight (Obedience of students and how they are forced to obey), but in this chapter it is going to be dealt carefully and fully so as to remind those section of students that alter the school laws. As I said in the said chapter, the law giver was the principal, the law enforcers were the school senior functionaries, while the law breakers were some students, especially class five students who call themselves senior students.

These class five students will never have the respect for school laws. They always went contrary to the school orders. This year, (1977), when the Head of State, General Olusegun Obasanjo, visited some schools in Sokoto State he gave one class five student twelve strokes of the cane for not dressing properly. Class five students were the source of evil in all secondary schools because it was from there that all the other bodies of students learnt their ways of life.

For example, the principal said things against harbouring of non-boarders in the dormitories, and even feeding them in the refectory by the class five students. He said that if they go unpunished that the class one students, when they reach class five, will say that when they were in class one that the present class five students 'harboured' some people in the dormitories, and that they themselves will do also. Likewise, when this matter was brought up by the principal, all that the class five students could do was to shout and make noise, whistling "Okongwu, anyi anugo"(Old man, we have heard).

They were the teachers of evil in the school. Instead of

upholding the laws and traditions of the school they destroyed it. They practised all sorts of mischiefs. They were warned many times by the functionaries and the staff (law enforcement organs) but they would not hear. There was never a time, as I heard in the history of the school, which stated that class five students ever wore the appropriate dormitory uniform. They wore mufti colours all around. They were reported many a time by the senior disciplinarian, and suspended many times by the principal but they would not hear. They think that they were still small boys that advice should be given. They were old and wise enough to think and do what was right and what was wrong.

They were the one who introduced 'expo' in the secondary schools. They gave the junior ones 'expo' to throw in for them during examinations.

The heartlessness and the brutality of class five students towards the junior students were causing great concern to the school authorities. They beat people like cows, and even if they were cows, they would eventually die off. They punished recklessly. They sent someone on an errand by force. (I remember one class five student who will never beg you to go on an errand for him but by force, and will even tell you the time to return, if not trouble will emerge).This inhumanity of class five students will be eradicated as the years were going on and things were changing.

Others will not concentrate on their studies for the fast approaching WASC, but will spend their leisure and non leisure time going to 'PMB' through the 'apian way', and drinking alcoholic drinks in the town. So class five students should beware or else evil will be onto them.

Another set of people that learned to alter laws were the small class one and two students. Their own misbehaviour lay in the question of fetching water to the kitchen. Some had formed the habit of 'dodging' in the bush when the fetching was going on. Some even sacrificed their food for fetching only a bucket to the kitchen! There was a time a group of students were suspended on the question of fetching water to the kitchen, yet they did not agree to comply. (Any class one student who makes himself known to the school authority as a bad boy will have a miserable stay throughout his mission in the school). There were some who intentionally throw their buckets or fetching vessels into the tank full of water because they did not want to fetch water, and they will use it as an excuse for not fetching water.

There was a night in which one boy engraved on the wall of the refectory some words which cannot be read at night because there was no light, but the boy wrote it with a torch. In the morning, about 6 am, I went inside the refectory to sweep away the last piece of food we had taken in the night. I was the first person to go there. At a side of the wall were written things like this.

Laws of Eating in our School
1. Blessed are the days we take yam 'poporopo' (porridge) in the morning for our white shirts will be ready to welcome the oil.
2. Blessed are the days we take rice, for our teeth will be struggling with grains of stones.
3. Blessed are the days we take beans for the result will be sleeping in the classroom.
4. Blessed are those that eat double plate for the result will be constant visits to the toilet.
5. Blessed are those boys who go back to the refectory to eat the grains of food that were on the table for they shall dwell in the kingdom of vultures.
6. Blessed are those that drink Omuo stream water for they shall have two things in mind; (1) the state of changing colour; and (2), the inheritance of guinea worm.
7. Blessed are the class one and two students that fail to fetch water for they will miss their food.
8. Blessed are the class one and two students who share 'partial' for their reward is exchanging of plates.
9. Blessed is the senior refectorian for he shall eat to his satisfaction.
10. Blessed are those class five students who harass sharers for

they shall have 'lion's share.'

11. And lastly, Blessed are the class four students who share food for they have initiated themselves into the 'Agu Ukpo'(gluttons) society.

Again, class one and two students who share food had always formed the habit of sharing 'partial'. They first filed their plates with food and meat before putting for others. This led them to be punished severally by the senior 'tormentors'. They were also fond of putting the greatest share for their so-called 'masters'. So, class one and two students should beware, or else they will get themselves into serious trouble.

The last set of people that their behaviour should be looked into are the class four students. This set of students were the main source of indiscipline in the school. They were the set of people who tried to overpower the students' regime.

One must look into what they usually did. They were the set of people that banned the use of one type of pant which they called 'Nwafor pant' with seven colours of the rainbow. During the assembly when the letters were being called out, if they hear any name ending with Nwafor, they will all shout, "pant!" If they saw any person who, by chance, wore the so-called 'Nwafor" pant,' they will start to shout, but thanks to the SP of 76/77 session for making it possible for the eradication of this silly attitude.

So, class four boys should learn how to behave because

Nwafor, Igba na enu
 Esom gi,
Nwafor, Igba na ni,
Esom gi,
Nwafor, nke na eku nwa,
Na be ndi ocha.

(Which means in English)

Nwafor, if you go up!
I will follow you,

Nwafor, If you go down!
I will follow you,
Nwafor that is
Keeping child
At the white
Man's place.

They also sang mocking songs at the person wearing it, and even threw stones and sticks at the person:

Who is the owner of this Nwafor pant?
Is it like yours?
Who is the owner of this Nwafor pant?
Is it like yours?
It is smelling badly
On me,
It is smelling badly on me

Chapter Eleven
The Great Inspection

Any of you who is reading this book and who has been to secondary school will know the emphasis placed on tidiness of the school compound or premises.

Around the dormitories you will see pieces of *garri* and rice all around the places. Near the refectory itself, it was even worse for a human being to look at. The principal had warned many times about this dumping of *garri* and other waste food in the school compound. Pits had been made for the purpose but yet some stubborn ones were still on the old practice. Water proof foil used to wrap bread will be seen in front of every dormitory you go to. Leaves used to rap *agidi* will be seen also. Any visitor who came to the school will think that it was not human beings who were living there.

So, one afternoon, on a Friday after school, the S.P. and other senior functionaries rang the bell so as to assemble all the students living in the boarding houses. When everybody came he said, "Good afternoon, students," to which we all answered, "Good afternoon, Sir."

He said that the principal, the assistant and the Dean of Studies had said that there will be a general inspection tomorrow being Saturday at about 9am in the morning.

He said that all pieces of things and parts should be cleared today as general labour, before the regular house work would be attended to. He said also that everybody must appear in his school or dormitory uniform tomorrow. He further warned that anybody found in any other uniform outside the mentioned one will find himself to blame. After he had finished speaking everybody dispersed.

Within a short time classes 1 – 3 students started appearing with their brooms and dust pans. Duties were allotted to each person who cleared his own portion immediately.

Back at our dormitory, our dormitory prefect gave about twelve boys the curtains to wash in the stream. Within a short time they returned with all the curtains. All the classes 1 – 3 students in our dormitory were asked to come outside for the cleaning of the outside of our dormitory. We came out immediately to do the work.

After the work, if you had gone round the whole compound it was good to look at now. All the parts where swept. Rubbish piles were carried away to the dumping pit. On the following morning, around 7am, everybody had taken his bath and put on his school or boarding uniform be he a class one or a class five student.

After bathing, everybody dressed his bed with white bed sheet, and the pillow with a white pillow case. The dormitory was thoroughly swept by four boys for about four times so as to make sure that no rubbish was found around or inside the dormitory. All the students who used wrappers to cover their beds hung them down.

All round, the dormitory was swept thoroughly by class one and two students. All the rubbish inside the basket were carried to the dumping pit for disposal. Around 8:30am the S.P and other functionaries went round the dormitories to tell students to stand by the side of their beds because the time was at hand for the inspection of the compound, especially the dormitories. About twenty minutes after his speech, the Principal came along with the Vice, and the Dean of Studies. They, first, went round the school compound before inspecting the dormitories.

After the inspection of the school compound they entered the first dormitory. As they went round they were recording what they saw. When they entered our dormitory, Ibiam, everybody stood still. They looked under our beds; and they shifted the lockers to see if any rubbish was there. To their surprise there was no rubbish to be seen. They looked at the dress of the students; it was all the same – white and white. The hair was combed and the shirts 'tucked in'. They entered the 'box room'; it was all the same. They went outside to inspect the surroundings of the dormitory. As they were going they were nodding their heads, writing something in the note books which they carried in their hands.

After the inspection of our dormitory they passed on to another dormitory near our own. At the left side of the dormitory there was a bed which was not dressed. (The owner of the bed went home and did not give anybody the key to the locker where the bed sheet was kept). As they were writing this, one boy jumped in through the window tying wrapper! (It may be that he did not know that they were in his dormitory, so he jumped through the window so that he could change his dress before they came), but unluckily for him the window in which he jumped through was the window in which inspectors stood. He was caught red-handed. His name was taken and he was ordered to meet the principal on Monday. It was also written down by the inspectors. The surroundings of this dormitory were fine but not to be compared with our own. They passed to the other two remaining dormitories, Onwe and Alinta, which were also as good as the dormitory in which the undressed bed was found.

After the inspection, the bell was rung so as to assemble the students inside the school hall for the result of the inspection. We all went to the hall, each person thinking that their house was going to win the contest. The masters inspecting the dorms took their seats. The functionaries held sticks in their hands so as to frighten the students who were making noise. At last there was dead silence in the whole place; people talking, talked in low voices so that they cannot be heard.

After some time the principal spoke. He said that "you knew what we came to do here this morning. It was to inspect the surroundings of the school in which you live. The result of the inspection is like this" (as he said "the result of the ...") we held our breath so as to know which house that came on top). "I – b – I – a - m house, first!" There was a shout of joy from the members of our house. After the shout he said "clap for them" – "kpa kpa – kpa kpa kpa – kpa!" "Onwe - 2nd, Ziks – third." He continued – till he reached the last house, Ikpenwa house, which came last. There were shouts of "uuhhuhu" from all angles (It was in this house that the undressed bed was found and also the person who jumped in through the window).

After the announcement of the results we all dashed out of the hall joyfully to do other activities in the school compound.

On the following Monday, during the assembly, the principal said many things about keeping the compound clean by students.

He warned that during any other inspection he conducted, if he found seeds of beans as was found in Ikpenwa hostel the last time, in any other dormitory, the members of the house, especially the hostel prefect, will be punished severely. As he was saying this, he called out the boy who jumped through the window. When the boy came out he explained the boy's offence to the students as a whole. He warned that students were not thieves that jumped through the window, whether pursued or not. He said that if any such act was committed again in the school that the offender will find himself to blame. The boy was told to lie down for his punishment. The boy who did not dress his bed was called out too. He was told to lie down too for his own punishment. The first offender was given twelve strokes of the cane as his punishment, while the second was given six lashes of the whip as his own punishment. After the exercise, the Senior Prefect came forward, said the prayers and the pledge. The song, "Loving keeper of thy sheep" took us into our classes.

The song rang like this:

Loving keeper of
Thy sheep, keep me,
Lord in safety keep,
Nothing can thy power withstand,
None can plough me from
Thy handle – Amen

With this song, we all marched quietly to our classes for the study of the day.

So ended the unforgettable inspection conducted by the Principal, the Vice Principal, and the Dean of Studies of the school, together with the Senior Prefect and the School Senior Disciplinarian which I had witnessed in the school. The inspection was really magnificent in the history of the school.

Chapter Twelve
1977 Independence Anniversary Celebration

This is the story of how we celebrated the independence anniversary of 1977 at Awgu. I had been to many independence anniversary celebrations but 1977's one was the most eventful I had ever attended.

It remained a week to the great day at the Awgu government field in which the Anniversary marking Nigeria's 17 years will take place. One day, after the assembly, instead of being told to march to our classes, the Games Master told us to group ourselves into groups just as we did during the last year's own. We did so without much hesitation. The functionaries were allotted to different groups to teach, together with some masters. Our group was group one or 'A', which was the group made up of small persons not above the height of 5 feet or so.

The person commanding us was the school senior librarian with two other masters. After some time he told us to spread with, "chest out," "stand at ease", "attention", "by your left", "mark time," "left, right, left right," and "forward march". Some were marching with little effort until they saw the games master looking at them. It was then that they started to march with full effort.

"Swing your arms," "chest out," "knees up," "short spaces in front," "left right, left right." And so it continued. With this command, we marched into the field where other groups or squads were already marching. We marched round the field about two times and were ordered out by our group commander into the assembly ground. From there we marched to our classes.

We continued to do this march past every day; each day putting on great appearances. On the last two days before the independence cerebration there was 'salute' in our school. We all marched into the field, as usual, but this time to salute so that they can know what our performance that day at Awgu would be like.

All the different squads took their positions until their names were called. "Squad One, come out and march so that you can salute," our commander said. "Hands on your neighbour's shoulders place." "Hands down", "Attention," "By your left, mark time," "Left, right, left right, forward march". We marched for about 10 yards when he said "left wheel, swing your hands."

"One, two, three, four, one, two, three, four, one, two, three, four." We changed, for as we were marching, we were nearing the saluting point. Then our commander said, "open order on the march, open order, march." "Check one, two, top, three + two, top, three, one, two, left, right, left, right." When we reached the place we were going to take the salute our commander said, "E-y-e-s Right." From now we were using slow movement until we passed the place. Our commander again said, "E-y-e-s front." We marched until we reached the assembly ground. Other groups did like this, and also marched to the assembly ground. After a small address by the principal we all marched to our classes to receive our normal lessons.

The following day was Friday, which was a public holiday, so the principal told everybody who had not washed his school uniform to do so in order to have them dry before that day at Awgu. That Friday, after the afternoon's meal, a great number of students were seen going down the stream to wash their clothes. After returning, they spread them on the grass, "praying" that the rain will not pour down. Luckily enough, the rain did not fall. That night the clothes were all pressed so that they will be fine.

On the morrow which was the great day, around 5am everybody was woken up by the SP and the S.S.D. for us to take our baths on time and wait for the bus our principal chartered for us. We did so, and instead of the food which was always shared at 7:30am, it was shared at 6:30am that morning. After putting on our white shirts and white shorts or trousers (but there were some who put them on temporarily for they carried with them bags which contained mufti dresses. They called themselves 'guys'), we waited for the bus.

At last, the bus arrived. Meanwhile, the school van was loaded with the junior players who were going to play with Mgbowo Boys Secondary School (I was once a player but I resigned because I was taller than the measuring stick by about two inches). We entered the bus, beginning with those who came first. Within a short time, the driver came and started the engine. We were soon on the move. When we passed about three poles, we started to sing in Igbo:

> Driver, give it speed
> Give it speed, driver
> Give it speed, give it speed, let- u-s
> G-o-o
> Driver, give it speed,
> Give it speed, let us go.

This we continued to sing until we reached the place.

We all jumped down, so that the driver will do more trips. After about five more trips, the whole students were at Awgu (except those that were 'dodging,' or those that were not well). In the trip, our senior team wore their new Jerseys and tugs and boots ('Red Devil'). The cultural dance troupe was conveyed at about 8:30am. We all marched into the field to take our stand like the other schools. When the D.O. or L.G.O. took his position, the Nigerian national anthem was sung:

> Nigeria, we hail thee
> Our own dear native land,
> Though tribe and tongue may differ,
> In brotherhood we stand.
> Nigerians are proud to serve,
> Our sovereign motherland.

After the song the band men started to beat their band, so that the salutation will be taken. The first school marched, followed by another school. Then, it reached our school. We marched as we marched in the school compound, and there was a loud clap of hands as we were saluting.

After the march past, the result was revealed which rang thus: "Awgu High School, Nenwe, first". When we heard this we all shouted with joy. Everybody now looked on the dancing groups to perform what they had in store for us.

The dancers showed great interest in their work. Some were acrobatic dancers who performed some 'magic' while others, mainly women dancers, were not all that great. We also came on top in the dancing and our dancers were televised on the T.V.

The third item was the match between our boys and those from Mgbowo boys. The match was an unequal one, as they were played half-field by our boys. When the match ended we defeated them by 2 – 0.

After the junior boys' match the rain started to fall, or to pour down. I could see those self-sufficient, ungovernable idiots who were putting on their gorgeous dresses and shoes called 'stiletto,' running for shelter. One of them was about to cross the pavement when he fell to the muddy ground.

After the rain, the senior boys went into the field to play. It was between our senior team and their Agbogwugwu counterparts. Our senior team wore their 'Red and Red', and their opponents wore 'blue and black.' The first half ended in a goaless draw. The second half opened at the height of our boys in their attack to score. Notable among the players were Iroko and Kakwe Brow. Our defence was tightened and our forward lines were also good. They made several attempts at the opponents' goal mouth but their goal keeper was a good goal keeper.

Our first goal came when our outside right crossed the ball and a header came from our inside left, which entered the net. Members of our school shouted with joy when the ball entered the net of our counterparts.

They passed the ball, and immediately the ball went near our goal mouth. My heart started to beat because I thought they will score. Immediately I was thinking this a shot came through but our goalkeeper got the ball. A free kick was taken by our left full back which went straight to the eighteen half of the opponents' side. Our centre forward beat a defender and was above to push the ball inside the net when the other defender seized his leg which made him to get small injury. The referee awarded our man a penalty kick which went inside the net.

They have scarcely passed the ball when their inside right played the ball to the outside left who, in turn, crossed it to the centre of our goal post. There was a tussle for the possession of the ball, and luckily for our opponents our centre three mistakenly played the ball inside our net. They played and played but no side scored any more goals. So, it ended 2-1 in our favour.

After the match, we all rushed to our bus which conveyed us to the school happily. After about four more trips all the members of our school who were at Awgu were all conveyed back to our school.

At school, the event was discussed by the members of our school, especially about the match and the person who fell sorrowfully into the muddy ground.

On Monday, the principal congratulated us for the performance at Awgu on Saturday. Moreover, he gave us three hearty cheers: "hip, hip, hip," "hurrah!" "hip, hip, hip," "hurrah!" and, lastly, for the people who took part in any sports that day, "hip, hip, hip!" "hurrah".

So ended the independence anniversary celebration.

Chapter Thirteen
Way of Life in Our School

If you are going to Enugu from Awgu, near Nenwe, on the left hand side of the road, you will see the sign board of our school as it stood gigantically. On approaching the entrance of the school compound, you will go a distance of about 120 yards 'avenue' before you could get to the school itself. The first building you will see is the school main building which was built of cement block but some parts are in a state of disorder because of its old age.

The main building comprised all the offices and about five classrooms. At the right side of the main building is the house of one of our masters (our Games Master), which is behind the new building for class one students. Near the new building is another building which is still being constructed. It is followed by the principal's houses which is in turn, followed by the other masters' house. Behind the Games Master's house is Alinta dormitory. Ziks dormitory is at the back of Alinta dormitory. Behind Ziks dormitory there is a path that leads to the engine house and the toilet and the bathrooms. At the extreme right of Alinta dormitory is Ezeanya dormitory which is the last dormitory on that side.

On the left side of the main building is the school laboratory. The main building is just in front of the laboratory and the class three and two blocks. Behind the laboratories is Ikpenwa hostel. Near it is Ibiam hostel which is in front of Onwe hostel. Side by side Ibiam hostel is Nwonye hostel. Near Ikpenwa hostel, on the left, is the school kitchen which is backed by the refectory and the school hall.

At the back of the hall is a path that leads to Omuo stream.

All around the compound are grasses which are cut low by students. There are paths which lead to every dormitory or hostel. All the dormitories or hostels are painted with red and green paint. Every hostel has its curtains for decoration.

The school was built in or around nineteen fifty-four. So the school is an old one. No wonder that the walls are cracking and fading because of their old age.

Life of Students

i. The students live their past life. There were some who were good and those that were bad. There were some who I did not think had all the necessary equipments for school life. For example, they had no spoon with which to eat which made them to remove another person's own. Also, there were some who did not have pens for writing. They would also take another person's own and call it 'tapping'. There were also other peculiar matters but the most dangerous was stealing. I don't know whether the school authority was very inefficient in finding out the person who stole people's money.

If your money was missing and you report it to the dormitory or hostel prefect all he would do was to call out all the students of your hostel and would tell them about the incident after which he will say, "If any of you know that he is with the money let him take it to the person you stole it from or to me." There were some who will pick people's things and kept them as their own. Does it mean that those thieves and pickpockets who always remove people's things, that their guardians did not provide them with all those things? Or did they sell their own? The answer cannot be easily answered but students must be warned about the way they behave, especially class five and four students.

Culture and Tradition

Almost all the culture and the tradition of life in our school had not changed. Normal life and activity continued as it was before but there were some or few which had been changed. All the students had the laws guiding them in the school from class one to class five. The laws must be adhered to but anybody who broke or altered these laws will find themselves to blame because of the punishment.

As I have said in the former chapters, the principal and the functionaries were the law enforcement agents while some students were law-breakers as a whole. Below are some of the traditions that must be looked into:

i. The tradition of "OBC" is still practiced in the school since its existence. OBC means, "Obey Before Complain," e.g. if a class four student was punishing a class two student, the junior boy or student must obey the order of the class four boy or student no matter what. If the senior released him he can report him to a higher authority, but if a senior student was punishing a junior student for supposed wrongdoing (sometimes for nothing's sake, for there were some who always did that) and the junior student reported him without doing the punishment, the case will not be settled. They would only tell him to obey before he complains to anybody or any person.

ii. In the case of water fetching to the kitchen, the tradition for the class one and two students fetching water is still in existence only that there was an addition to it. For example, class three boys were fetching now. I don't know whether it was because of shortage of water or because of what, or whether it will continue until about three sets of class three students had fetched to the kitchen. (You should note that in the case of fetching water to the kitchen, that the helpers of functionaries, the junior refectorians, those that were not mentally well, and the junior players when the time for match was at hand, were excluded from it). The punishment for not fetching water to the kitchen was either that your food will be seized, and your plate also seized, or you will fetch thrice the number of buckets others had fetched before your food will be given back to you.

iii. The culture or tradition of the class one and two students who find themselves attached to the class five students or help the class five students was still in practice. When the class one students had returned, senior boys will ask them, "who are you helping?" If the person said that he was not helping anybody, the questioner will tell him to follow him to his corner where he will tell him to start helping him. But if he asked the person who he was helping, and he replied that he was helping so and so boy, if the class five student knew the person he will leave him, but if not he will question him again. If the boy explained well the questioner will leave him and seek for another person. This he will continue to do until he found one person.

iv. The question of class 1 – 3 students working during the evening in the boarding house was still in practice. All the students of classes 1 – 3 will, on Tuesday and Thursday, around five o'clock in the evening, assemble in front of the labour prefect's cubicle or hostel for the evening work. This work was compulsory except those that were not well. The supervisors of the work were the class four students, if the WASC was nearing, but if it was in the first term, the supervisors will be class five students.

v. The last point about the culture and tradition that will be touched on was the question of class 1 – 3 students reading from 7:30 – 9:30pm. Classes 1 – 3 students will, after eating about 7:30pm, go to the class for night prep although some stubborn ones, called 'ndiochie,' still remained behind. They always find themselves being punished thoroughly in the assembly.

Chapter Fourteen
Evil Days in our School

I should say that my first term in class three witnessed some evil days in our school. Below were some happenings which proved this saying to be true in the real sense of it.

i. **The Removal of the Windscreen of Our Principal's car**

   On the day we came back from the long vacation to start a new academic session, students were horror stricken to hear that thieves had moved in the night to steal the back and front windscreens (glass) of our principal's car. This was how it happened: our principal had returned from the small leave the government gave him on the day the school reopened and just parked his car in a place made for the parking of the car. It was in the evening, so he went into his house to rest. In the night he went to sleep, only to wake up in the morning to see that thieves had taken away the front and back windscreens of his car. It looked as if the thieves scraped the rubber used to protect them with a sharp pen knife. As they were doing this thing the school night watch man saw a glimpse of them and started chasing them. They ran with the windscreens into the bush.

   In the morning, the school bell was rung to assemble all the students. When we came, we were marched to the bush in which they thieves were pursued to. We saw footsteps really. We searched for about one hour without finding the windscreens which we thought were buried somewhere in the bush. We searched, again and again, without finding them, so we went back to the school compound.

Meanwhile, reports were made to the police at Awgu who found one of the culprits. Later, two others were caught and detained also, but since then we had not heard anything about them.

ii. **The fainting of one of our students**

Because of lack of accommodation for class one boys' classrooms, the principal made available a place at one corner of the refectory for class 4A students. He gave a strict warning that no student should be found eating there. He warned that anybody caught would find himself to blame. After school the class 4A boys entered and arranged their new classroom, and wrote on the black board with a white chalk, "We are not aware of your class, so if you mess up we treat you like a kid." This, they inscribed in big letters.

In the night, after sharing the food, one class five student (I don't know his aim), went into the classroom with some other boys to eat their food. When he was eating, mistakenly his soup poured on the black board which fell on the ground. The SP told the boy not to do that but in the eyes of the class 4A boys it was not satisfactory. After eating, about twelve of them went into the hostel of the boy to drag him out so that he will clean the blackboard. When they reached to drag him out, he refused to go which earned for him a serious and fierce beating with sticks. One class five student who wanted to fight for his mate held one class four student in a tussle. The brother of the class 4A boy told the class five student who held his brother to leave him. As he was saying this the friend of the class five student came and held the other boy. As they were doing this, a fierce fight broke out. They carried each other to a person's bed and fell upon the tent. The boy who owned the tent was angered by the deed. He removed the broken tent and lashed out at the two boys fighting. As he did so, the lashes hit one of the class four students who dropped on the ground and fainted.

The senior prefect was called who, in turn, called the principal and the vice principal. When they came, they examined the boy, and found that the top of his head was pushing up and down, in the way of breathing through the head. A towel was tied to the wound and he was driven to the hospital in the van of our vice-principal, in the shower of heavy rain. At Awgu hospital the boy did not receive treatment for the doctor in charge of the hospital was not there. When they returned, a student who knew how to drive was contacted and, with the SP and some other boys, they drove to the Enugu hospital (UNTH).

Two days later the boy returned, very well. The case was judged and those involved were sentenced to two weeks suspension.

iii. Thieves Broke into our Cook's Store Room.

One Tuesday morning, about four days after the incident of the fainting of the boy, members of our school were shocked to hear that thieves had broken into the store of one of our cooks – the place in which he slept. This was how it happened. On Monday night he had gone to sleep as usual, not thinking of any evil befalling him. It was a rainy night so everybody went to bed early. His place was some distance away from the school compound. Around 1:30am in the rainy night, the thieves came. Because of the rain he did not know when they entered because the store was built of 'zink'. With a knife, they broke the 'zink' door and went inside. They woke him up with a whip on his buttocks. When he woke up they fired a gun at another place so as to frighten him, for they did not want to kill him that particular time. They told him to lie down, again, with his face downwards. They also took his money, gave him a beating with their guns and rod, but when they raised their machete and brought it down on his head he was prepared to die. Luckily for him, the knife touched the iron bed before descending on his head. When he saw his blood rushing out, with all his strength, he pushed the man at the door back, who fell on the sandy ground. He picked a bottle and blasted the face of one of the thieves. Then, he started running. They fired another shot but because of the night they did not get him.

iv. **Mad Woman Devastating the School Main Building's Glass Window**

We returned to find that a mad woman was destroying the glass windows and doors of the school main building. Nearly all the windows were destroyed before we returned from the cross country race. When we returned, we encountered her with stones and clubs. When she saw that it was useless to run away she, with a small dagger, cut deep into the side of her ear to claim that it was students who did that but that did not stop the matter. The students kept on throwing stones at her until she fell on the ground. Clubs were applied but without success. The students continued hitting her on her legs and hands until they were sure that they were broken but the woman did not move. Instead she passed away waste product on her clothes. The school van was sent for. When the principal came, the unconscious woman was carried in it to the hospital.

V. *Snake Entered One of the Dormitories*

We were in the class only to hear that a snake had fallen from a tree top and entered into one of the school dormitories in the night. A search was conducted, but no sign of the snake was seen. In the morning, the snake raised its thirsty mouth to strike one boy who was quick enough to escape the bite of the dangerous animal. Searches were made again, but without success. Up till today, the snake had not been seen or killed.

Article for the School Magazine
The Mystery of the Virgin Forest

This story took place in the far north of the neighbouring clan, where the people also worship the great god who was the sole proprietor of the beautiful, modest and virgin forest. This magnificent, mysterious and disastrous god had a beautiful daughter who was dazzling in the morning sun, charming to the naked eyes, and notorious in the mind.

The chief priest of the god had constantly and ingeniously warned the clan members not to dare enter the forest to cut trees or farm. Roaming about in all the forest, and serving the man and his daughter were the young Thetis of the deep seas.

Appearing in the farm in the morning sun, wearing a costly embroidered cloth, carrying a bunch of wild leaves, and dimming the eyes of the early farmers, was the daughter, Mbibele, who was nearing her prime age. She was beautiful in appearance, gentle in walk and unhurried in her behaviour.

The farmers took cover under the shade of the great *Ichekuru* tree whenever they saw the glorious, climatic and high royal blood of the young queen.

The adherence to the law of the god was stable for he had the ability and undertaking of a conquering mind. The peaceful atmosphere created by obeying the rules of the great Mbide was violated and polluted by a greedy, selfish, obstinate, and stubborn man who caused great stir and sensation in the whole clan one early morning. By so doing, he pulled down the wrath and the anger of the god who vowed vengeance, revenge and woe, and almost killed innocent men and shed a very great costly blood.

In the early morning of the fateful day; when the morning sun was just piercing the cracks in the thatched walls; when the fowls were just coming out from the pen; when most eminent and able tappers were setting out for their palm trees; when old women were going in and out from their houses, carrying away old ash; and when children were rolling out of bed, stretching themselves, and with water pots, finding their way to the stream, this man made up his mind to tempt a great, outstanding evil.

The fate and the gallantry of this man was a beautiful story told in the affected place.

Reaching the forest, this man, without fear, went to the palace and the cave-like abode in which Mbide and his daughter were living. The man was indeed great, brave and fearless to withstand the awful smell of the virgin forest, around which roamed unknown figures, and also the revolting smell of human blood devoured by the supernatural, immortal and spiritual beings.

The way to the palace was crooked, and covered by fearful, awful smelling flowers, and covered by human parts for medicinal and occult purposes. Around a great pool of water, surrounded by young maidens, who held washing instruments, and all who were ebony black, attractive, and had piercing eyes, was the queen who was bathing in the pool. When the man entered the place, all eyes were set upon him. When he saw the queen, the flash he received was enough to withhold a man doing what he intended not to do. Her charming nakedness, her full, maturing breasts thrusting upwards, her plaited hair styled with dangerous herbs, and her fingers, all shone in the sunlight which almost blinded the man.

Half blinded, half confused, and half ashamed, the brave warrior, with this machete, came out through the thick covering of the maidens, and lo! up went his knife and down upon the hair of the queen. Within a short time the other maidens were lying helpless and hopeless upon their face downwards. The queen, before she died, spat out a dangerous curse, telling the man if he did not carry her to her father that the evil that she spat out shall follow thee. The man, amazed, astonished, surprised, frightened, and partially fearful, instead of carrying out the order, fell upon his own machete and died.

In his glorious manner, the king, rising from his noon day rest, suspected that an evil deed went on at the pool side. There, he saw the damaged sight of his most beloved, most respected, most adored, most charming lady — daughter in a pool of blood, killed by a mortal beast. From there he ascended to the sky, appeared at the centre of the clan's *Ilo*, and wrapped himself in a thin mist, covered by smoky fiery cleavages. He thundered, so that the earth shook.

The horror-stricken people of the clan turned into a tumultuous and stampeding force when the roaring sound was heard. As a punishment for the acrimonious and unbelievable deed, Mbide cursed all the palm trees to wither. Weaklings and even limping old men also came to see the great demon and maniacal angel. The chief priest cursed and shouted taboo words, and summoned the half-alive and half-dead people to the *Ilo*.

There, still wrapped in the mist, was Mbide, forsaking and ignoring the pleas and sacrifices of the chief priest. The god sent a terrible wind, a gale of hurricane power over the land and vowed to crush the family of the man. Every year, he will take one beautiful woman in place of his lost one. But this did not end the matter, for the ghost of the queen was constantly doing damage, demolishing and destroying valuable lives, and also shedding human blood until a vigorous god offered to fight with Mbide. It was a decisive battle for which every ear that heard it twinkled, and every eye that saw it cried out tears.

As the battle went on, all the creatures created by God cried out in alarm. Also, the scorching heat of the two powerful gods raged here and there. They fenced and pinned themselves with herbal medicines and 'ebang' of the wonderful power. The new god had dignity and cunning, and nimbleness won for him the great contest, as no breathing creature had ever seen and heard. With the latter god's great herb which overwhelmed and overpowered the former god's overlordship, Mbide was weakened, and was changed in to a thin figure which soon escaped into the thin air.

Mbuki, the new god, cleared the forest, destroyed the wonderful shrine of Mbide, and placed himself as the new outstanding and good ruler of the people.

Although free, the thought of Mbide always remained in their minds and made them start. The thought also penetrated into their nerves, their navel, and their nervous system. The great episode was still remembered in the place, and small children refused to go to the back of the house so as to keep away from evil spirits. The insect Mbide was changed into became a great obstacle to the people until Mbuti used courage and mystical mind to wipe him out from the face of the spiritual world. Yet, the damage done by the demented and deathless spirit, though he had vanished, was beyond repair.

The question of its image appearing to the mind of many people remained obscure. The power of positive thinking was used to overcome this thought in the mind of many people. But there was even a rumour that Mbide always appeared to many people in the night while they were sleeping, and caused bloody nightmares to the people concerned. Whether this was true or not, it was uncertain, but the remembrance of such great appearances of the stubborn and obstinate devil came in many versions.

Appeals were made to Mbuki who said that all was well, and that nothing about Mbide would be heard again, but they didn't know that Mbide had changed from being an insect into the ruler of the Nri-dwarfs in a very distant place.

They constituted themselves into a well formed metallic, medicine group to recapture the forest and install him, once more, as the ruthless, dreaded and witch-like king. The Nri-dwarfs performed every kind of magic; they had gone deep into Okpo and knew almost all the herbal leaves in all the surrounding areas.

They waited for the most convenient time to launch their attack in the forest. The king of the forest was not taken unawares but was prepared, renewing his medicine before they can strike at his den. In the battle, the whole trees in the ground near the battle field fell off from their roots. All the animals and human beings trembled, and the forest shook in silence to the ravaging destruction and evil deeds done by the leader of the Nri-dwarfs. It was a decisive battle, for it will decide who should rule the place again. The new leader was the victor. The head of the Nri-dwarfs vanished because all his combatants had been destroyed and killed in the grim struggle.

ANECDOTES, RECOLLECTIONS AND REMINISCENCES ON THE MAKING OF AN INTELLECTUAL ICON OF OUR TIME – UDENTA, O. UDENTA

BY

PATRICK ISIOGWU

It all began in the mid 1970s (June/July, 1975), when we all came as fresh students to Awgu High School, Nenwe, formerly known as Awgu County Secondary School, the premier secondary school in the Colonial Awgu Division. The school was founded in 1957 in the old Eastern Region of Nigeria, and is currently in the present Awgu Local Government Area of Enugu State.

When we all got enrolled as fresh students then, hardly did any of us know each other so well or our exact mission, but we all relished the euphoria of being admitted as secondary school students. In those days this meant a lot to both parents and wards, especially as the names of successful pupils in the Common Entrance Examination to secondary schools were published in the Regional/National Newspapers then, under the secondary schools they were posted to.

Today, everyone knows this intellectual Icon/dynamite of our time as UDENTA, O. UDENTA.

However, it is noteworthy that during this early period when we all arrived at Awgu High School, Nenwe, he was simply known as LAWRENCE UDENTA.

From simply Lawrence Udenta to Lawrence O. Udenta and, after about two years into secondary school, the nickname "KILL MASTER" crept in, to almost replace LAWRENCE O. UDENTA.

How this nickname of "KILL MASTER" crept in is what I do not know till date except that I must state here that the nickname threatened to completely obscure his name at Awgu High School, Nenwe because while it was easy then to know/identify "kill master", the majority of the students had completely forgotten his real name then as LAWRENCE O. UDENTA.

While his first name LAWRENCE gradually and effectively

disappeared from his names, UDENTA which apparently was his grandfather's name, was not difficult for him to adopt as a replacement to his first name as his own father was known as MR. BENEDICT UDENTA.

Till date, many do not know/understand what the initial "O" stands for in his name. The "O" simply stands for "ONWUAMAEZE in Igbo language, which translates to in English language, "Death Does Not Care About Your Status As a King." It is from the foregoing that the names, UDENTA O. UDENTA came about.

As earlier stated, when we all started at Awgu High School, Nenwe in mid 1975 as fresh students, not much was known then of anyone, including LAWRENCE UDENTA or simply LAW as he was then called.

He (LAWRENCE UDENTA), had two elder brothers then at Awgu High School, Nenwe as he was the last born in a family of four. The other two elder brothers were far more popular than him then except that after some two to three years in secondary school, his own hurricane-type of popularity began to emerge powerfully.

While his most elder brother – Maurice UDENTA, simply known then as MOO UDENTA, was one year our senior in the school and known for his interest in sports, especially football and social events/fashion, his immediate elder brother who was in the same class with us, was BENEDICT UDENTA (JUNIOR), who apparently goes by their father's name and hence the (JUNIOR) after his name.

This, his immediate elder brother – BENEDICT UDENTA (JUNIOR), was the one you cannot fail to notice anytime, any day, both for the right and wrong reasons, as he was both vibrant and voluble, and perhaps 'stubborn'. He courted controversy and seemed not to get enough of it. It was like he simply enjoyed a tensed atmosphere then. He made his marks in academics but conceded that his junior brother – LAW Udenta was simply in a class of his own. This same Benedict Udenta Jr. also made his marks in sports and, infact, was appointed the school's sports prefect in our set.

UDENTA O. UDENTA, then Lawrence O. Udenta, hails from Mgbowo in the present Awgu Local Government Area of Enugu state, and is the last son and child of his parents among three others – two elder brothers and one sister.

He is presently married to Mrs. Vivian Udenta and blessed with a lovely son – Master Chidera Udenta.

As earlier stated in this short piece, this man of letters/ideas UDENTA O. UDENTA was not quite visible academically or otherwise when we came into secondary school as fresh pupils, and nothing at the beginning alerted us (his classmates) of his enormous potentials as his size or academic performance during the first two years into secondary school was of no note, and as such no one looked at his direction as a threat on the academic sphere.

The students that were academically very visible and seen as outstanding right from our first year were the late Peter Chike, Richard Uwakwe, now a Professor of Medicine, Simon Agu, the late Christopher Aju, Augustine Umahi, Edwin Chukwu, Emmanuel Akpa, my humble self (at the risk of being immodest!), Benedict Udenta Jr and several others.

However, by the time we got into our third year, and by the end of year four, Lawrence Udenta had emerged from nowhere not only as a threat to the already known names but simply came to challenge as the foremost student academically. No one was prepared for the contest, and unknown to so many students he was over prepared, as the unfolding events proved when he emerged on the secondary school academic scene.

It was like he used the previous three/four years to read and research into every academic field, and some of the manifestations and encounters (episodes) discussed here attest to this fact because by then he was simply unstoppable. Infact, by then, he was already an avant-garde of sorts.

The very first was his performance during the school's debates (he was a member of the school's debating society) and other numerous debates in the evenings after school hours.

It was during one of these debates that he brought a dimension and presentation that left everyone gasping for breath as his diction and overall performance was not anything known to the students and teachers alike. One particular single performance in one of the school's debates opened everyone's eyes and alerted all discerning minds about the presence of a budding intellectual colossus.

One of the immediate fallouts of his electrifying performance in that debate was that one of my town's boy by name Frank Mbanta (not real name), came to me by night time to lament that the performance of Lawrence O. Udenta not only overwhelmed him but that he was completely demoralized to continue his secondary education, complaining to me about the oratorical prowess, confidence, and authoritative approach of a classmate in marshalling his points. He also told me that the worst was that it came to a point where he (Frank Mbanta) cannot even understand/comprehend the words of somebody who was supposed to be his classmate. He insisted on throwing in the towel.

After his narration, I simply consoled him and pleaded with him on the need not to drop out of school on the account of the performance of Lawrence O. Udenta. I felt distressed and outraged by the emotions of this particular student who happened to come from the same town/village with me but there was not much I could have done other than the advice/plea I made to him.

On another occasion, during another debating session/episode, Lawrence O. Udenta so much elevated the subject of discourse to a pedestal that was far removed from the students and got the atmosphere charged/electrified with so much facts, figures and references to several authorities in order to buttress his points that at a point, one of the leading lights (academically) in our set – PETER CHIKE simply rose up and called on other students to disrupt/boycott the session. He told everyone present that Lawrence O. Udenta was only debating with himself as there was no one present who can counter all he (Lawrence O. Udenta) has been saying as his references/examples on the subject were drawn from China, Soviet Union, Canada, United States and other far flung parts of the earth. Indeed, it was more of a lecture than a debate.

By then, this student – Peter Chike, informed the listeners that their biggest handicap and dilemma was that apart from the fact that they cannot counter the position of Lawrence O. Udenta on all the issues, no one was sure/aware if he was not even telling the audience lies as everyone was simply cheering on. That was how that session ended.

It also emerged that after our fourth year, with one year to finish our secondary school education, Lawrence O. Udenta effectively stopped attending all classes for the fifth year. When some of us who were close to him inquired from him why he refused to attend classes, he simply said to anyone who cared, that, "the only difference between me and the teachers is that they have written their exams."

What this means was that he, (Lawrence O. Udenta) had nothing to gain academically by attending classes as he felt convinced that he had already covered enough academically not to bother about what was being taught in the class then.

During this period, we used to have what was known as "Auxiliary Teachers" – those who just finished their secondary education but, because they were extremely gifted and made good grades in their West African School Certificate Examination, they were recruited as teachers to teach in secondary schools those days. This may well be the category of teachers he was referring to then.

It was also during this period that the idea of writing came to him as he also told anyone on inquiry, including me, that rather than come to the classes to learn 'nothing', as he stood to gain nothing, he would rather concentrate on writing novels, poems, etc. It was this period that he actually started writing in earnest. He also revealed to some of his contemporaries that he had already covered (studied) the syllabus for all subjects for our West African School Certificate Examinations one year before the examinations and had no challenge in that direction. Thus, he started writing (books, novels and poems) in his secondary school days, which came in his later life to define the essential UDENTA O. UDENTA.

At this point, his fame in secondary school had overtaken him such that during one class session (English language), a student who could not properly comprehend the English Teacher was directed by the teacher to see Lawrence O. Udenta, who was not in the class at the time of the lecture for proper understanding of the lessons. For some of us in the class, this was quite embarrassing, added to the fact that the teacher did not seem to bother that this particular student was not even in the class for learning.

Another episode worth recalling was how Lawrence O. Udenta was the leader of a group of about four students that pleaded with our Literature master, one David Iliyasu Dhacko, a native of Niger State posted to our school then as a Youth Corper, to help us cover our syllabus for the West African Examination Council one year ahead for the reason that he the (teacher) was good at the subject and there was no guarantee of getting another good teacher in the final year. This teacher then asked how he was going to do it, and he was told to simply get the books in the syllabus for **WASCE** 1979/80 and summarize them during lesson sessions. This made half of the students in the class to simply abandon Literature in English as subject of study as they felt they could not cope with the system of study the teacher was plodded to adopt.

By the time this particular teacher was leaving our school at the end of his one year service, being also the end of our fourth year in secondary school, he assured that anyone (students) who made at least 60% in his exam should be sure of making an 'A' in school certificate examinations in this subject.

True to the words of this departing Youth Corps teacher, by the first term of our class five when another teacher came to teach literature, he was so overwhelmed by the performance of some students during the first term examination in class five that he scored some students so high that this even elicited murmurings from the concerned students. In this first term examination, one Christopher Aju scored 96%, Lawrence O. Udenta scored 95% and Patrick Isiogwu scored 94% in the literature examination. As usual with this elite group, they normally brought together all their marked manuscripts for post mortem analysis.

On this occasion, Lawrence O. Udenta did the analysis on these three best scores. He pointed out the unique angles each of the three students answered the questions. On the manuscript of Christopher Aju who scored 96%, he remarked that what made the paper unique was that it was apparent that he (Christopher Aju) memorized the entire William Shakespeare's *Macbeth* as he quoted extensively from it in his answer sheets, including the pages and lines within the pages of the book, and that was why he had the highest score of 96%. On that of Patrick Isiogwu who scored 94%, he noted that the manuscript was unique in the choice of words (diction) and overall organization. On his own paper where he scored 95%, he noted that it drew heavily from that of Christopher Aju and Patrick Isiogwu, and concluded that since all of us had known the strategy of Christopher Aju, he should brace up for competition as that was the last time he was going to score the highest in the subject.

Another notable experience was the advice of our History Teacher to the same Lawrence O. Udenta after our first term examination in class five. The History Teacher, after the review of his answer sheets (manuscripts), cautioned him that though he scored the highest in the subject that he should endeavour to curtail the level of his presentations and the language employed to deliver them, considering his age and the examination (**WASCE**), he was about to sit. This advice to Lawrence O. Udenta came about because, according to the History Teacher, Udenta's presentation was too far advanced and above what was expected at his level, and efforts should be made so that his final results (**WASCE**) were not seized by **WAEC** on the grounds of suspicion of cheating it being external examination where his academic antecedents were not known to the examiners.

Along this direction was his penchant to always be the first to finish the writing of his papers (exams) in a class/set made up of 250 students, at least, 30 minutes before the end of the time allotted for the paper. When some of us felt concerned, we cornered him to know why he was always in a haste to finish his papers (exams) ahead of every other student in the examination hall. We also wanted to make him understand the necessity of reading through his answers even if he finished ahead of every student but he simply retorted "that it was unnecessary, as reviewing his answers will still discover no error in the paper for the examiner to find out". And this was happening during the **WASCE** that was taken so seriously by all the students.

It was this state of affairs that made him to always stand in the midst of students after each paper (exams) to give answers to questions just finished in the examination hall, especially the objective questions that had optional answers of A, B, C, D. He used to be so authoritative as to what constituted the correct answers such that at a point, he will simply be telling the crowd of students, "If you did not give this particular answer you have failed it". At this stage, I fled in order to retain my sanity as long as the examinations lasted. I did not want to stay at these post mortem sessions and probably hear that I did not answer any question correctly as it may affect my subsequent performance in other papers by unwittingly inflicting some psychological trauma on myself.

Another compelling episode was his encounter with the school authorities at Awgu High School, Nenwe which was an exemplification of the mindset of an accomplished activist. This encounter was to later define his future life in the area of human rights and civil society platforms.

This encounter came about as a result of the bad feeding condition the entire boarding students of the school experienced then, that resulted to a loud murmur which almost snowballed to a crisis. The situation arose because the students were fed with beans in the morning, in the afternoon and in the evening of the same day, and some students grouped themselves under the aegis of G. 11 (mostly the elite students) to confront the school authorities on this sordid state of affairs.

However, when the situation became very tense and the school authorities threatened reprisals, all the other 10 students in the G.11 fled, backed down and pledged their undiluted loyalty to the school authorities thereby leaving only Lawrence O. Udenta as the only non-conformist among the students. He decided to go solo instead of backing down and living with the shame of attempted capitulation.

By this time, the Principal of the school then, Mr. Timothy Umeukaeje, had brought a written query with the letter head of the then Anambra State Schools Management Board seeking explanations on the conduct of the students that threatened some actions if their bad feeding conditions persisted.

On the strength of the Principal's query, Lawrence O. Udenta generated 18 pages of his written reply which he sent to the principal of the school and copied to the then Anambra State Schools Management Board. In Udenta's written reply, he raised several fundamental questions concerning the absurdity of feeding the students for the whole day with only beans, magnifying the health hazards that could result from that; the fact that the principal's private food store was full of different varieties of food stuffs; and other general lapses in the overall running of the school. It was a monumental indictment/embarrassment to the school authorities.

This written reply from Lawrence O. Udenta, not only unearthed several issues being glossed over, it completely embarrassed the school authorities such that a middle of the ground solution was sought to resolve the matter. This was facilitated by one of the senior teachers (Dean of Studies), Mr. Obi Okafor, who initiated a private meeting with Lawrence O. Udenta where he conceded that, indeed, the issues raised in the 18 pages reply were valid but pleaded that it should not be pushed too far in order not to create the impression that the school's authorities capitulated before a small boy. He promised to set in motion measures to remedy the bad situations. Almost immediately, the school's food store was supplied with different types of food stuffs and there was a manifest improvement in the overall welfare of the students.

The final encounter on this episode was at the school's morning assembly ground with an elevated platform, where the Principal/Teachers stayed to address the students. It was at this elevated platform that the Principal of the school called up Lawrence O. Udenta and pointedly said to him: "I heard that you were planning a riot?" only for Lawrence O. Udenta to fire back at the Principal by asking, "Sir, if I was planning a riot, how come that the students did not riot?" At this point there was a thunderous ovation by the entire students (over 1,000 students) of the school of "KILL MASTER" that rent the air which got the Principal of the school bemused. After the massive ovation for Lawrence O. Udenta had died down, the Principal remarked that the school would not condone the activities of "radicals and pocket lawyers," and told Lawrence O. Udenta that any future occurrence he the (principal) would report the matter to his father and that was the end.

While there were several other remarkable recollections of that era that later defined the essence of the man –Udenta O. Udenta, it will be impossible to put all of them down in this short piece which is not intended to give a comprehensive picture but an overview/insight into what defines the man from the early stages of his life. It is impossible to fully examine the essential Udenta O. Udenta here as that is not the intention, especially his humanism, the self-made man that he is, and indeed as a man of destiny. This account is only a glimpse as to when, where and how it all started.

It is only fair to record that because of his excellence academically, he was appointed the school's Study Prefect, and also a member of the students and staff (school management) consultative forum for the well-being of the school. Immediately we finished our WASCE, he gained admission to the University of Nigeria, Nsukka to continue his studies and later at the University of Benin for his graduate studies, and continued further advanced studies/researches.

While at the University of Nigeria, Nsukka as a student, he was the leader of the Marxist Youth Movement. He became a lecturer at the Federal Polytechnic, Oko and later moved to Abia state University, Uturu also as a lecturer. From there, he became a member/Director Publicity and Strategy of Eastern Mandate Union, a member NADECO and became very visible as an activist and a pro-democracy campaigner of that period. He was later detained/imprisoned along with Dr. Author Nwankwo, the Chancellor of Eastern Mandate Union by the General Sani Abacha junta.

He regained his freedom following the death of General Sani Abacha and joined the democratic forces to enthrone democracy in Nigeria. He was the founding National Secretary of Alliance for Democracy. He has since held several positions both in the Public and Private domain in Nigeria, including the positions of Director in the Institute for Peace and Conflict Resolution The Presidency, Abuja and as Director-General of the Presidential campaign organization of a former presidential candidate and now a Senator of the Federal Republic of Nigeria (Sen Bukola

Saraki), as well as a Deputy Director-General of the Presidential Campaign Organization of Atiku Abubakar, Nigeria's Former Vice-President.

He is a commentator/analyst of repute on National and International affairs, and has travelled far and wide all over the globe, including the United States of America, United Kingdom, The Netherlands, New Zealand, Germany, Switzerland, Australia, France, Ghana, Belguim, Austria, Singapore, UAE, South Africa, Ethiopia, – etc. He listens to classical and operatic music, especially when in his massive and well stocked/appointed library/study.

PATRICK ISIOGWU – is UDENTA O. UDENTA's Secondary School Classmate.

www.ingramcontent.com/pod-product-compliance
Lightning Source LLC
Chambersburg PA
CBHW011947150426
43193CB00019B/2928